220.972
Sa44b

CONVENT OF THE SACRED HEART
EL CAJON, CALIFORNIA

CHRISTIAN HERITAGE COLLEGE LIBRARY
2100 Greenfield Dr.
El Cajon, California 92021

CONVENT OF THE SACRED HEART
EL CAJON, CALIFORNIA

BUILDERS IN THE SUN
Five Mexican Architects

Juan O'Gorman

Luis Barragán

Candela

Mathias Goeritz

BUILDERS

IN THE SUN

CONVENT OF THE SACRED HEART
EL CAJON, CALIFORNIA

Five Mexican Architects

By CLIVE BAMFORD SMITH

Foreword by Dr. José Villagrán García

ARCHITECTURAL BOOK PUBLISHING CO., Inc.   *New York*

CONVENT OF THE SACRED HEART
EL CAJON, CALIFORNIA

720.9
S644

11033

Copyright © 1967 by Architectural Book Publishing Co., Inc.

All rights reserved. No part of this book
may be reproduced without
written permission of the publisher.

Published simultaneously in Canada
by Saunders, of Toronto, Ltd. Toronto 2B.

Library of Congress Catalog Card Number: 66-27873

DESIGNED BY AL LICHTENBERG

Printed in the United States of America

720.9
S644

Contents

31336

FOREWORD

by Dr. José Villagrán García

I T was Esther Born who published, in 1937, the first English account of the Mexican architectural movement, in a book entitled *The New Architecture in Mexico*. Since that seemingly remote year much has happened. Governmental and private construction has been abundant, and very different in character from that of thirty years ago.

Obviously, Mrs. Born did not expect to find, in Mexico, architecture so profuse or so frankly Western in character. It is interesting to reread the first page of her book, because it reveals the attitude of the foreign observer — the North American observer particularly — toward our ignored culture and the realities of our daily life. "Perhaps, to a large extent," wrote Mrs. Born, "this myth is still true, but it is contradicted, for instance, by René d'Harnoncourt, whose report concerns a peasant woman who is eager to exchange her Indian jug of incomparable design for a red gasoline can, which she covets, partly because it is scarce, partly because it is light, tough, durable, smooth and shiny" and "the value of a collection of buildings such as this one lies, then, not in the fact that Mexicans follow a different pursuit, but that they are engaged in the same pursuit as ours. . . . The point of view is familiar, but the accent is different. . . . We may try to estimate, if we wish, what they have lost and what they have gained."

It can be deduced that the mentality of the foreign observer at that time — a mentality which has not changed fundamentally — could not conceive that a country such as ours, economically weak and all but ignored in most aspects by the Euro-American West, should be in step with what was believed by Europeans to be their so advanced thought, achievement and accomplishment, and even should be doing things with a "different accent." I do not know what lasting effect the book produced, but I recall that it led to the publication, by specialists, of very varied opinions. Some, because they contemplated us from lofty ivory towers, openly expressed their failure to understand what we were doing. Others became interested for different reasons, similar to those indicated in d'Harnoncourt's anecdote, but so far as the red gasoline can specifically was concerned they were attracted merely by the different, and to them curious, approach that could be exploited.

It is clear that as of the end of the Second World War, Western Europe, drained of blood and avid for new vistas, different from those offered by the civilized barbarity in which it had for years cloaked itself, but moved also by the need for liberation from the egocentricity in which it tenaciously persisted and for markets which so far had evaded it, began to show an interest in Latin America: particularly in

Mexico, which, understandably, began to be rediscovered in its rich historical and cultural aspects, among which its architecture and painting are outstanding. This is not to say that Western interest in our enormous archeological treasure had been lacking. European and North American investigators, after all, together with a few Mexicans, began, at the end of the last century, to search for, to preserve and above all to study our pre-Hispanic and Colonial archeological sites.

The evolution of Western culture in all its manifestations inevitably has had repercussions both in Mexico and among those who observe and judge us from abroad. I would venture that what has most interested us in our architecture has been its progress, the service it renders to the national community by interpreting its multiple requirements, be they elementary economic or hygienic needs, or the esthetic aspirations which throughout history have been more important to us than mere comfort. It is easy to demonstrate that the innate inclination of our people toward the esthetic, in everything we do and the manner in which we try to live, is perhaps our chief characteristic.

I should like to examine, in very general terms, the perspective that our architecture offers. I recall various opinions which were expressed by foreign architects when they visited Mexico for the first time, in 1952, to attend the Pan American Congress of Architects. Some of them, confronted by basalt walls of considerable thickness and height, and pavements of the same material, the rough surfaces of which differ so greatly from those of the granite or polished marble floors which the European and North American are accustomed to tread, were unable to conceal their astonishment and revulsion at such manifestations of "barbarity" — the only term they could find to describe such treatment of basalt. In fact, this treatment stems not only from secular tradition, but also from the high cost of working such hard rock. Moreover, the use of such tri-dimensional qualities satisfies our idiosyncrasy. Many others shared these opinions, and it would be interesting to record their names now that, in their work and their criticism, they extol the quality of what they then called "orgies of color, incomprehensible to any sensible Western architect." Later, an

excellent architect from Philadelphia, contemplating the fronton courts of our University City, said that he waited, horrified, half expecting to see warm human blood trickling down the walls. Viewing various other University buildings, he dismissed them disdainfully as "clichés."

Various currents of thought were revealed. Some visitors brushed our work aside simply because it was — as it still is — regarded as regional. Others classified it as a simple imitative cliché, a copy of what was being done "everywhere." In fact, how could the adopted gasoline can be peculiarly ours, and why has the beautiful jug been exchanged for that practical, and to us potentially beautiful, receptacle?

The attitude of those who watch and study us has, indeed, changed little, if at all. A former student at the Bauhaus lamented recently that our architecture has lost most of the qualities which he appreciates in our past. But such people overlook the fact that our identification with Western culture is not new, has not been artificially pursued since our modern movement began some fifty years ago. Even to imagine this is to disregard our history. In the sixteenth century we were conquered by Spain, then a most powerful nation, which incorporated us into Western culture and baptized us "New Spain." The transfer of a culture to our country led to the formation of a new, Mexican nationality, and at the same time established the bases of a culture which, born of the West, grew up speaking its own accent: the "different accent" of which Mrs. Born wrote, and the "own accent" noted by Don Juan de la Encina, the Spanish historian and art critic who spent the last years of his life in Mexico, and came to affirm that we speak Castilian, but with our own accent, and attach different meanings to some Castilian words.

If it can be demonstrated that a Mexican accent was to be detected in our culture and in our architecture, identified as they were with the West, it remains to be proven that this accent still exists, and that it has not changed substantially, in tone, during at least the past four centuries. If no change has occurred, we must ask ourselves whether this tone or constant is rooted in our nationality, in the broad sense of the word. Only a positive answer can reveal the presence of a Mexican quality in our architecture, a quality which indeed exists, despite efforts to classify our work as a whole as "international," after a series of disorientated solutions had been applied to its problems.

On innumerable occasions, for decades, we have affirmed in our teaching and at international meetings that a common denominator, a native accent, can readily be identified in the outstanding architectural works of our rich history, a foundation of which we have built in this twentieth century. This accent is most clearly visible in popular architecture, including the modern, and manifests itself, sometimes ostentatiously, in construction of little or no esthetic value.

Since the appearance of the well known study "Invariantes castizos de la Arquitectura Española" ("Constants Peculiar to Spanish Architecture"), by the Spanish architect Chueca Goitia, diverse Mexican invariables, constants of our own, have been discovered within our multisecular architecture. There has been no lack of critics who qualify these factors as myths that cannot be sustained in the face of ideas now in vogue.

For my part, and with all due respect to these important studies, I have only cautiously surveyed the potentially fruitful field, peering out and catching on the wing, as it were, evidence that might be substantiated by even a cursory examination of the history of our building. The discussion has been enlightened by several distinguished colleagues. Suffice it to cite and recommend the more recent relative works: *Maya,* by the architect Pedro Ramirez Vazquez (1964), and the very interesting study published by the architect Ricardo de Robina in *Revista Arquitectura* (1963). These, and others, offer abundant information, and consolidate the belief that our Mexican constructions do incorporate constant characteristics.

The affirmation in turn leads one to ask whether what is observed by investigators or architects finds theoretical support in ideas current in the fields of culture and of anthropology, and can be explained as substrata of ethnic complexes or even of a multiplicity of historical fact, possessing such strength and persistence that they flourish despite the contradictory intentions of many recent and modern architects. Several of the architects who were charged with the erection of our important historical monuments were born or educated in Spain or elsewhere abroad, and the trend has continued in recent decades. Others by conviction have joined the ranks of the international movement, or have followed currents instigated by creators belonging to milieux very different from ours in their social, economic and cultural structures. Nevertheless, their works embody these constants or invariables, and bear also the seal of regionality, born of economic and climatic conditions which in too many cases still are being brushed aside or underestimated.

Every point on which we touch really requires amplification disproportionate to a brief survey. Even so, it seems indispensable to consider the possibility that this common factor exists and that it springs from our national history and characteristics, rising above the individualistic or non-national impulses of the architect at a time like the present. I should like to quote one of the world's outstanding humanists, Erich Kahler, of the Universities of Vienna, Heidelberg and Munich, Professor at Cornell and at Manchester, England. Speaking on the subject of "The True, the Good and the Beautiful" at Ohio State University in 1959, he commented that within the confines of human history not everything is pure change. There exists, he said, an element of consistency which runs through perpetual change, woven into it like a musical theme.

"The difficulty is — and this results from the great, perturbing difference between ancient and modern points of view — that we cannot separate the constant from the changing, that we cannot distill it from its living, historical substance. The constant exists only in its inextricable, joint function with that of change. This is valid for the particular qualities and values of nations, just as for what we call the character of a person, and, I assert, is equally true of man as a being, as an organic form. It is accepted and recognized . . . that any individual possesses a characteristic identity which implies particular ways of behavior, predilections or aversions. . . . The problem leaps to the eye when we consider a nation . . . because we have been educated to accept only the positive and scientific values, and to assume that only that which we can touch with our senses, directly or indirectly, really exists."

Kahler concluded that although our experiences have destroyed our faith in integral absolutes — that is to say in entities and values that could be valid for all times and all places — there still exist for us certain relative absolutes, valid within the confines of a particular human form. In every respect they are limited but dynamic absolutes. He affirmed that despite the evolution of a culture, an element of consistency remains, inextricably interwoven with the elements of change. The constant factor, in our case, would be the form or figure, inspired by and even intentionally copied from Spanish forms or, today, Western and universal forms.

If the theme of constant factors or invariables invites a series of discussions or objections, a comparison of the more characteristic architectural works of the moment with the constructions that inspire them reveals an overriding Western influence. Any notable difference can result only from regional influences.

As of the end of the sixteenth century, for multiple economic and political reasons, the pre-Cortesian form was abandoned, and was supplanted in our architecture by a new form which was Spanish in intention but not in fact. The native workman, and those who functioned as architects, proceeded to subject the genuinely Spanish forms to regional demands, imposed by historical, and no less by economic, climatic, geological and political considerations. It is sufficient to remember the fortress-convents of the sixteenth century, whose design coincided with the Spanish, but differed from it in many respects. The character of these beautiful, sturdy buildings relates them more to the forms they supplanted than does their ornamentation, for all its strong Indo-Mexican nature.

During the three centuries of Viceregal rule, the form inspires the figure in constructions modeled on Spain, but their size and resultant proportions, their three-dimensional qualities and their properties of light are unquestionably Mexican.

As one example among thousands, consider the tiny Oaxacan temples of Tlacochahuaya, where dimensions and the use of light are de-cidedly regional, but at the same time coincide with those used in other areas, where form, proportion and the nature of the materials used differ. Tonantzintla, in the State of Puebla, is without a doubt under the rule of a Mexican constant.

In brief, the figure, in the architecture of the Colonial era, does not coincide with that which preceded it in pre-Cortesian times. Nevertheless, it mysteriously conserves a strength of space which makes the dimensions of plazas and patios totally different from those built by the Spaniards from whom its form is copied. The patios of the Viceregal Palace or the Plaza de Armas, in Mexico City, or the main plaza of the town of Cholula, for example, present a sense of proportion that compares with the pre-Cortesian spaces achieved at Teotihuacan or Uxmal, but not with that of the Plaza Mayor of Madrid or of Salamanca, nor with the patios of an infinity of Spanish cloisters and palaces. All their distinctive qualities, throughout the three centuries of Colonial rule, strike a note which can be discerned nowhere except among us.

As our culture becomes more closely identified with the West, our architecture undoubtedly loses originality of figure, but the different use of size, light and proportion remains constant and, to paraphrase Kahler, becomes woven into the element of change.

The phenomenon of how, as quickly as we become incorporated culturally into the West, we tend more and more to neglect the figure while cultivating the other three qualities can be explained by the fact that an architecture transplanted to new surroundings can the more readily conserve its basic or national character while losing its intellectual and social identification with the community which imposes it or freely gives it its formal architectural orientation.

This, in effect, has happened in Mexico since the end of the sixteenth century, and continues to happen in these times in which, despite our architects, our total identification — factual, not merely verbal — with the West still is only half accomplished. Indeed, the mass of our people is unaware of it.

Our contemporary architecture, in its more genuine, more skillfully conceived achievements, acquires a seal which almost unwittingly is more and more widely recognized, and is related to that "relative absolute," the constant within evolutionary change that is intentionally orientated toward the universal level it might one day reach.

Our desire to be identified as Occidental accounts for the fact that our architecture today presents the same diversity as is found in the rich and powerful United States of America and, indeed, wherever Western culture flourishes. Thus the tendency to build glass cubes, to focus attention on outer surfaces so as to obtain an effect of spaciousness. However, tradition is causing a reaction against the type of structure of which architects, landlords and occupants alike seem to be tiring.

The frantic but fruitless pursuit of innovation finally obliges the pursuer to take refuge in ranch houses and other forms which typify our rich historical tradition. These forms, interpreted according to the dictates of fashion, yield, I think, examples of skillful scenography, picturesque buildings well worth analyzing even though they are inconsistent with the concept of an integrally conceived architecture.

Alongside this antiquated traditionalism, as it might be called, another nationalistic tendency is to be observed. It is characterized by an attempt to resolve the integral, multiphased architectural problem as it is related not only to form or esthetics, but also to economic and social considerations, and it ignores egocentric preoccupation with the probably outmoded avidity for originality. Such construction, which tries to serve the community, reveals a wealth of good intentions coupled with modesty of appearance, and for that reason does not seem to interest critics or commercial magazines, being so obviously related to our real problems, basic and pressing problems which normally are of concern only to us and, among us, to only a few. When such problems are resolved by the erection of modest rural schools or homes that truly help the community, little credit generally is given to those who build them or pay for them. There remains the harvest of gratitude of a community whose dissatisfaction has been heeded and attended.

One is told that a poor people is dazzled by ostentatious building. Doubtless this is true, but it is also certain that to waste time and talent that could be used to attack some of the people's monumental problems is socially unjustifiable. The almost brutal contrast between the ostentatiousness of many public buildings — and even more numerous private ones — and the stark fact of our poverty causes one to wonder, uneasily, how the two extremes can exist side by side.

Much would have to be written on so profound a problem. For his part, the architect here and everywhere else who sees himself obliged to work within a community in which such contrasts exist can find them stimulating to the extent that they represent reality, however harsh and painful it might be.

To return to the currents in the theory and practice of our architecture: apart from the present national tendency of which we have spoken there is another, similar one that is boundlessly individualistic. As in other countries, especially the United States, it is characterized among us by adherence to the teachings of new creators of forms, forms which seek originality rather than any overall solution to local architectural problems. Whether or not these posturings are of any worth in the plastic sense, they provoke heated criticism even among their practitioners. In countries such as ours, burdened with difficulties, they have not emerged from the fashion schools, even though some of their results are scattered about the country.

The qualities which flourish among the multiple tendencies and orientations we have surveyed possess a peculiar character. External appearance adheres to the model which inspired it. Be it actual or archaic, it acquires its own personality and even, in some cases, relative originality. The "accent," but even more the other three qualities we have discussed, serve to reassure the creative worker. The element of size and proportion that is proper to us is present in a multitude of compositions: in the new Anthropological Museum, the Tlaltelolco development and the University City, for example. Our uses of light, even in the glass cubes which resemble the uncounted thousands of their counterparts elsewhere, are unmistakably Mexican, emphasizing brilliant colors and contrasting tones such as those which typify our monuments and the small towns that still retain much of their enchanting eighteenth-century appearance. The Mexican usage of the tri-dimensional sense of space can be discerned in much of our present work, in tactile surfaces but more especially in habitable spaces, patios, corridors, terraces, walks and courtyards. The play of depth and light embodies, but does not coincide with, that achieved in the remote past.

Because they so clearly speak with their "own accent," these qualities can be picked out in numerous homes, churches and industrial buildings. In the University City, the Library, with its external murals, and the Stadium are two magnificent examples of this accent, because of the treatment of stone, of color, of textures and volumes. Dimensions and combinations which put down their roots in Mexico yet at the same time appear to be occidental are present in a multitude of other constructions.

An answer to the last question, as to what we might have gained or lost by exchanging a beautifully designed jug for a gasoline can, could lead to a restatement of what we have already set down. Our identification with the present and with the West obliged us to abandon the neo-academism of the last century, with a view not to innovate but rather to solve our most pressing problems, to build and to express ourselves in accordance with the demands of our collective and therefore national

existence. The transition from the exotic archaism which predominated until the beginning of this century to the regional archaism that unsuccessfully sought to revive what exists only in the works of the past, has been no mere snobbish gesture: nor was the rejection of an archaic-nationalistic concept. The transition led to the first attempts to work in the present, but within our tradition, and to our emergence in the 'twenties as a movement as much incorporated into the West as our own Mexican-Western culture in fact can be.

We must not, cannot, retreat from reality as a whole, nor from the facts concerning our architecture. We cannot fail to prove the existence of the Mexican accent that persists, regardless of our desire to keep pace with other advanced countries. Nor can we refrain from lamenting the neglect of our great national problems, in so far as they touch upon our mission to build appropriately, to build well, with close regard for our collective social, economic and esthetic needs. A perspective of unsuspected depth and breadth unfolds itself to the new architecture. Thoroughly and scientifically must we investigate the whole complicated range of problems that the Mexican offers to his architects, at least to those who feel themselves called upon to serve their fellows truly and unselfishly.

Our expression of the art of architecture has a great future open to it.

Juan O'Gorman

JUAN O'GORMAN

"Most architects are mere businessmen," huffs Juan O'Gorman. "Architecture today is based on a commercial proposition and, in turn, on the average, conformist taste of people who can afford to build: a boring situation, indeed. In 1938, as I did not know where to turn from functionalism, and as I had no intention of becoming a businessman, I abandoned architecture as a profession, and became a painter."

Among the multitude of his mural and easel paintings is the triple self-portrait at right, executed in 1950. "The pigeons all carry messages: even the toad brings a message," he recalls. "The butterflies and other insects are purely decorative and, for the information of people who construed their presence to mean that I am a naturalist, that's not a squirrel perched on the shoulder of the architect O'Gorman. It's a *diablito* — a little devil — whispering into my always receptive but sometimes puzzled ear."

Smiled the critic Raul Flores Guerrero: "Juan is a good painter and a rebellious, good architect. This is exceptional in Mexico, where good painters no longer abound, and rebellious architects simply are not supposed to exist."

BORN in Coyoacan, a leafy suburb of Mexico City, in 1905, Juan O'Gorman was educated in Jesuit private schools. He graduated from the School of Architecture of the National University of Mexico in 1927, having worked successively, during the last two years of his studies, with three prominent architects — Carlos Obregon Santacilia, José Villagrán García and Carlos Tarditi.

O'Gorman was "obsessed with the idea of building new houses, for the new life of the new society," by applying the theories advanced by Le Corbusier in *Vers une Architecture*, a book he had read four times during his nineteenth year. Between 1928 and 1937, he built a dozen functional private homes, including a house and studio for the painter Diego Rivera who, in later years, was to declare him "a complete master of the plastic arts." During four of those years, as Chief Architect of the Department of School Construction of the Secretariat of Education, he also designed and built some thirty primary schools and one technical school in Mexico City and a primary school in the Gulf port of Tampico.

All these buildings were planned and completed within the theory of strict functionalism. They were directly and obviously derived from Le Corbusier, although the planar surfaces were sometimes relieved by cantilever projections and exterior spiral stairways, and the glass areas offset by planes of blue, red, yellow or brown. They are still recognized as the first functional constructions to have been done in Mexico.

"But I realized long ago," O'Gorman muses, "that it was unfortunate that Le Corbusier, and not Frank Lloyd Wright, caught our attention. Wright would have helped us to stay closer to our true American tradition. He was the supreme architect of this century. He conceived the truly organic architecture of our time. Many of his buildings, definitely influenced by ancient, pre-Hispanic Mexico, are the best examples of American architecture. His house, Taliesin, is the greatest modern house built in this century, and is one of the most important works of art of all times. It has a recognizable Mexican character. It revives the Meso-American tradition. It was Wright, a frequent visitor to our archeological sites, who understood organic architecture as related to the human

being in his geographical and historical content. I find it deplorable that the pre-Hispanic influence is not visible in the architecture of modern Mexico."

No school of modern Mexican architecture exists, O'Gorman insists. "There are only three examples of modern Mexican architecture — the sports stadium and the fronton (jai-alai) courts at our University City, and my own home. What is called modern architecture has accumulated its esthetic baggage from a jumble of geometric forms. It ignores tradition. The International Style has become one of the most fatuous expressions of our uncivilized times. Architects are under the delusion that by applying one or another familiar formula they can achieve architecture of quality. Let's leave aside, for the moment, the fact that our real need is to house enormous numbers of people in comfortable, economical, functional and healthy surroundings. Purely mechanical functionalism, developed into modernistic architecture, can only produce mechanically 'artistic' effects and fashions which become ever more commercial, ever more unsightly. This International Style is well named. The people who require it and pay for it — and their architects are not free from blame — are precisely an international set with no sense of tradition and no artistic judgment. The humanist essence of architecture is being relegated to mere business interests. Nobody even bothers to look at the newest of these glass and concrete monstrosities, into which cold, heat and light enter with equal belligerency.

"Speaking of belligerency," he grins, "please believe that mine stems from sincere conviction. Functional architecture is a necessity of these times of population explosion. The principal social function of the architect, the builder — better call him the engineer of edifices — is to plan and build functional abodes. This is not the best solution, but it is today the most practical one. At least, mechanical functionalism is not a fashion. It is the objective and correct method of bettering the material conditions of the enormous numbers of people who need housing, schools, hospitals, in greater and greater numbers and volume. The need for art in architecture remains, but under the pressures of this age we cannot make it a universal condition of architecture, least of all in

Juan O'Gorman in the patio of his home.

the innumerable underdeveloped countries.

"Functionalism has been distorted in practice. The theory might be reexamined, properly formulated. Architecture must become a work of art, an expression of man's deepseated need to achieve harmony with his surroundings and with his fellow men. Functionalism became, in Mexico at least, the antithesis of the plastic arts. The characteristics of Mexican architecture are the pyramidal form of the composition; the dynamic asymmetry of the axis; the complex variety of the decoration; richness of form and color; the superb manner in which the building can harmonize with the landscape. We can't hope to solve our mass housing problems and at the same time build in strict accordance with such principles — not immediately, anyhow. But let us make a beginning."

The University Library

Juan O'Gorman planned and built the Library of the National Autonomous University of Mexico in 1950, and in 1951-52 designed and constructed the mosaics that cover the four sides of the ten-story tower of closed stacks.

Initially, he planned it as a building of volcanic rock, with insloping, terraced walls, and windows of translucent onyx in the shape of a truncated pyramid. It would have resembled the ancient pyramids of Meso-America, but its design differed too radically from that of the University City as a whole.

Reading rooms occupy the two lower floors. Book stacks for nearly a million and a half volumes are enclosed in the air-conditioned tower.

The mosaics cover 4440 square yards. They are composed of some three million stones, each less than two inches in diameter. They constitute a history of ideas in Mexico, portraying the pre-Hispanic past, a world of magic in which arts and sciences were developed and demonstrated to a stage still almost beyond belief; the European past inherited from Spain; and the effect of both periods on modern Mexico.

The architectural historian Henry Russell Hitchcock commented that "O'Gorman has used the walls of the stack tower, unbroken except by tiny windows, like the pages of an illustrated codex. The colors of the mosaic are remarkably soft and rich, while the scale and texture is definitely architectural."

North wall (longer) and west wall of the Library of the National Autonomous University of Mexico.

South (larger) and east walls, University Library.

South wall, University Library.

South wall (larger)
and west wall,
University Library.

The face of the Aztec Rain God, Tlaloc, "a piece of pure Pop Sculpture," according to O'Gorman, looks out over a shallow pool from the base of the University Library.

Details of colored stone mosaics on the south wall of the Library. The theme: the conception of good as brought and imposed by the Spaniards. Ptolemy believed the earth was the center of the universe and the sun revolved around it; the Spanish Church inferred that man therefore stood at the center of all creation. This period in Mexico's history was marked by the building of innumerable churches and the flourishing of the Cross. It resulted in the death of Aztec Emperor Cuauhtemoc and the collapse of the religion and civilization he represented; O'Gorman depicts the defeated Emperor (bottom center) hurtling to his end.

Detail of mosaic, east wall of the Library. The dove of peace surmounts a concept of the ➡
splitting of the atom. Themes of industrial and civilian building are pursued below.

Detail of stone mosaics on south wall of the Library. The conquering Spaniards erect their
churches atop the ruins of Aztec temples and pyramids, and create new symbols of eccle-
siastical and temporal authority.

The Mexican Revolution begins, spurred by the slogans of "Long Live the Revolution" and ➡
"Land and Liberty."

O'Gorman's Mosaics

Mosaics should be treated as an architectural theme, in O'Gorman's opinion. "They bring us into the realm of color as a part of architecture, which in antiquity and until the Renaissance was an essential part of the composition. It has been our good fortune, in Mexico, to initiate the movement to reincorporate painting and sculpture into architecture."

O'Gorman observes that Antonio Gaudi used ceramic mosaics as a necessary complement to the baroque forms of his great architecture, and without them "would never have achieved, for instance, the snakelike balustrade in the Parque Guell, in Barcelona."

He is just as enthusiastic about Fernand Cheval, the French postman who decorated his homemade castle with oyster shells, broken pottery and colored glass; the builder of the Watts Towers in California; and Raymond Isidore, keeper of the Chartres graveyard, who covered his Chateau des Assiettes Cassées, and even his furniture, with mosaics. "These breaths of freshness and creation are a wondrous relief in the stagnant academic atmos-

O'Gorman's colored stone mosaics at the entrance to the Secretariat

phere of our pretentious, commercial times," he declares. "They reveal the love of decoration which is the beneficent characteristic of the baroque, and incidentally is inherent in our Mexican tradition. Baroque is the only word to describe the multitude of possibilities of an architecture using mosaics, whether on the surfaces of walls or ceilings, or as a permanent form of polychrome sculpture."

O'Gorman completed his colored mosaic "Homage to Cuauhtemoc," at the Hotel de la Mision, Taxco, in 1957, and in the same year he began the mosaics that decorate the entrance to the Secretariat of Communications and Public Works in Mexico City. In 1963-64, using natural colored stones found in Chile, he constructed a large mosaic, called "Fraternity of the Indo-American Peoples," at the Tupahue public swimming pools in the Parque San Cristobal, Santiago.

"The stone mosaic of natural colors is more appropriate than the classic mosaic of colored glass, and much less expensive," says O'Gorman. The way to construct them was discovered accidentally, during the building of the Anahuacali, Diego Rivera's Muséum of Ancient Mexican Sculpture in San Pablo Tepetlapa, Mexico City, in 1945-46. Stone was the only material found to be adequate for facing the concrete slabs. A bed of broken stone was laid on the wooden forms before the concrete was cast, and a facing of stone chips was given to the concrete surface when the forms were removed. "This led to the making of elementary designs with different colored stone chips and obtaining, as on the ceilings of the Museum, regular, decorative mosaics. So far as I know, these natural-colored stone mosaics were the first to be made in our times.

"The same technique was used at the University Library. Natural-colored chips of stone were set onto a drawn pattern of about one square yard, each a tiny part of the total composition. A slab about two inches thick was produced by reinforcing and pouring the concrete. These prefabricated slabs could be lifted by two men, and were fixed to the building after the walls had been waterproofed."

of Communications and Public Works, Mexico City.

Mosaic "Homage to Cuauhtemoc" at the Posada de la Mision, Taxco.

Birds, a serpent and various animals native to the region are incorporated into the colored mosaics that decorate the upper terrace of the house.

O'Gorman's Home

"This house, built on the rocks of the Pedregal of San Angel, is the most complete and satisfying work that I have done in architecture," O'Gorman avers. "It is an example of Organic Architecture, and I think it can be called modern and Mexican.

"Organic Architecture produces edifices which, on account of their form and color — as works of art — achieve harmony between man and the part of the world in which he lives, between the forms of the buildings and the landscapes surrounding them. Also, it continues and develops building tradition, although it does not copy the form of archeological architecture.

"I set out to make a house that would fit esthetically, harmoniously, into the landscape of the lava formation of the Pedregal, and to express the tradition of the ancient architecture of Mexico, as distinct from the Spanish and other Colonial styles imported from Europe. The house derives its Mexican character and its human root from this continuation of our tradition."

From the air, the lava of the Pedregal resembles a sea of stone, curved like waves. The plan of the house follows these naturally formed curves. From the ground, the lava presents a series of aggressive formations that stand out in rugged, stark shapes, and the house shares this characteristic. It is built of the lava stone on which it sits, and is incorporated into a cave formation of rock. Mosaics of different colored stones form reliefs on the outer walls, and merge into those which decorate the living room.

"The mosaics are reminiscent, chiefly, of the vegetation and the animal life of the Pedregal," O'Gorman comments. "Year by year, the house becomes more entwined in its natural landscape, because of the harmony of form and color."

The landscaping is the work of Mrs. O'Gorman, née Helen Fowler of Seattle, Washington, who has made extensive use of plants native to the Pedregal. A sculptress who worked with A. Archipenko in Chicago, Mrs. O'Gorman also does fine and exact paintings in dry water colors. Her book *Plantas y Flores de Mexico* is profusely illustrated with her paintings.

CONVENT OF THE SACRED HEART
EL CAJON, CALIFORNIA
11033

Upper terrace of O'Gorman's home in the Jardines del Pedregal, San Angel, Mexico City. The fanciful bird, in yellow, red and black mosaics, performs a useful function: "It is a wind-breaker," O'Gorman explains.

Year by year the house becomes more closely identified with the gardens and lush vegetation that surround it.

The lava rock from which the living room is carved, and on which the rest of the house sits, and of which it is all built.

A skylighted grotto in the living room of the house. The ceiling mosaics are a sea of symbols, mostly Aztec. The animals moving across the wall of the grotto are jaguars, monkeys, squirrels and others more difficult to identify. A brilliant blue and scarlet butterfly is almost as big as the jaguar.

Color mosaics decorating
the ground floor exterior
of the O'Gorman house.

Another view of skylighted grotto shown on page 37.

Detail of exterior mosaic.

Cantilevered staircase to the upper floor of O'Gorman's home.

The School of Industrial Techniques, planned by Juan O'Gorman, under construction in 1935, Mexico City.

House O'Gorman planned and built for a noted North American writer on Mexican folklore, Mrs. Frances Toor, in Mexico City, 1935.

Two views of the house O'Gorman planned and built for his brother, historian Tomás O'Gorman, in San Angel, Mexico City, 1931.

First house of Juan O'Gorman in San Angel, Mexico City, 1932.

Two views of one of the first houses built in the now sprawling Lomas de Chapultepec residential area of Mexico City. It was planned and built by O'Gorman in 1928, when he was an
enthusiastic believer in the Le Corbusier theory of functionalism, for Ernesto Martinez de
Alba, a prominent engineer.

House built for the painter, Julio Castellanos, Mexico City, 1934.

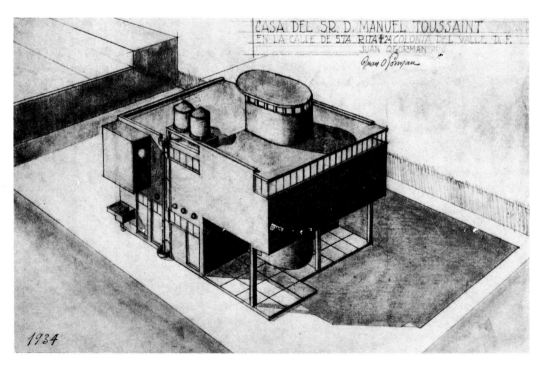

A functional home built for Manuel Toussaint, Mexico City, 1934.

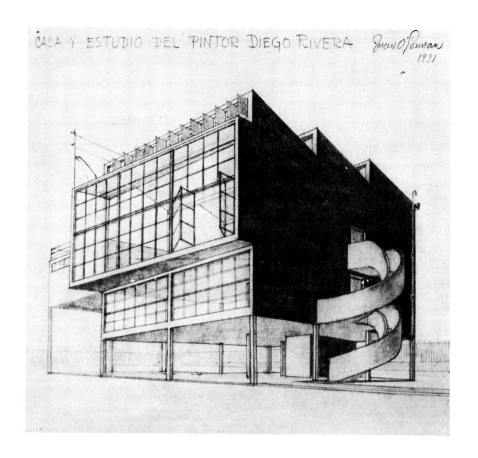

Two views of the house and studio O'Gorman built for the painter Diego Rivera in San Angel, Mexico City, 1931.

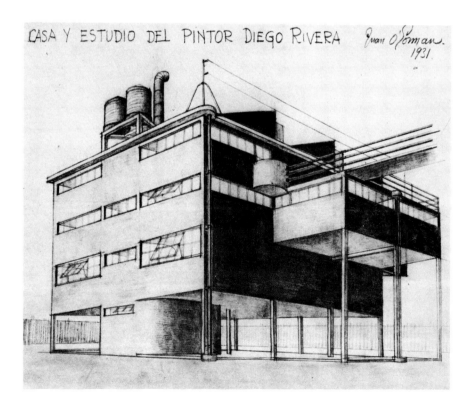

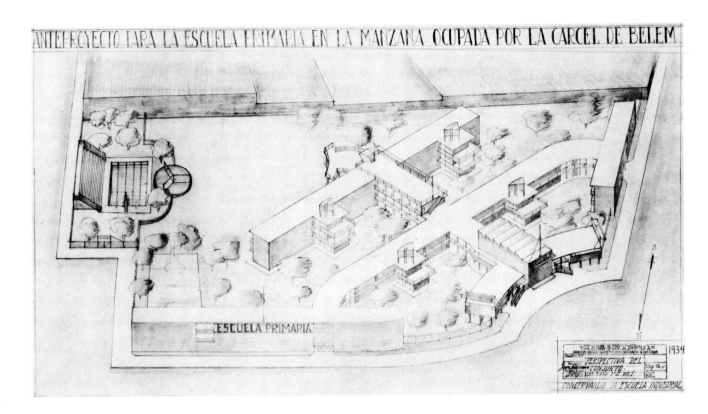

One of the many primary schools designed and built by O'Gorman in Mexico City during the period when he was Chief Architect of the Department of School Construction of the Secretariat of Public Education.

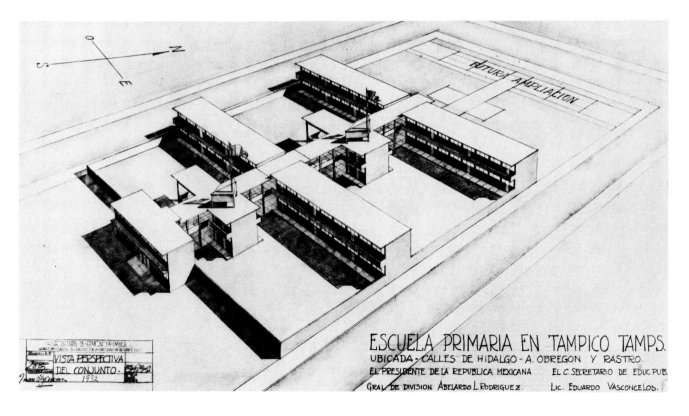

A primary school built in the port of Tampico, 1932.

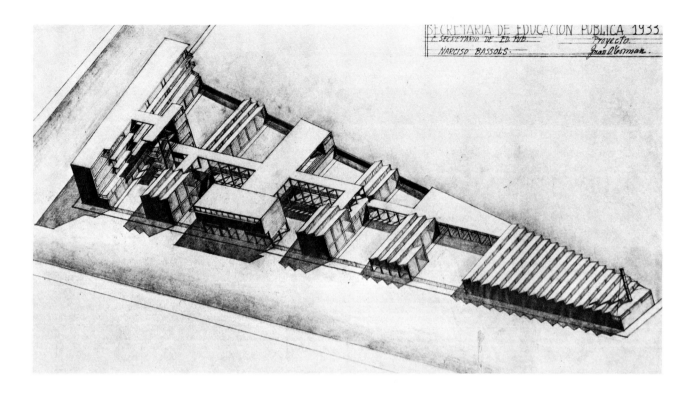

The Technical and Vocational School for Men, Mexico City, built by O'Gorman in 1933.

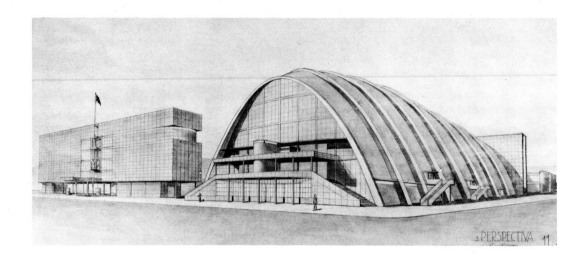

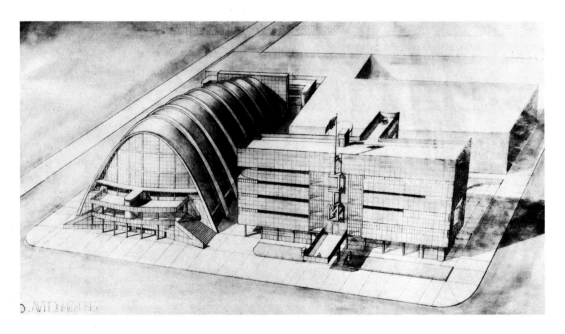

Three drawings made by Juan O'Gorman for an office-auditorium for the Mexican Confederation of Labor (CTM) in 1934. The project was not completed.

Luis Barragán

LUIS BARRAGAN

From boyhood to early manhood Luis Barragan, born in the provincial capital, Guadalajara, lived only for the long family vacations on a widespreading cattle ranch in the mountains and lush valleys where the States of Jalisco and Michoacan meet. As he grew up he spent more and more time in the outlying areas of the ranch, where the horse was the only means of transportation. The beauty of those mountains, woods and vales, and the sturdy simplicity of the rustic architecture of the region, ever since have been reflected in his work, and he remains an accomplished horseman.

He did not glimpse Mexico City until he passed through it in 1924, on his way to Europe, where he traveled almost constantly for two years, losing the interest he had shown in civil engineering but gaining a knowledge of architecture and its history. When he returned home he devoted two years to designing and constructing houses before he was obliged to take an active part in the administration of his family's ranch and farm properties. He spent another year in Paris, in 1931-32, attending Le Corbusier's lectures and seeking out the writer and landscape architect Ferdinand Bac. The time he could spare from the study of Le Corbusier's theories and methods was spent on the Riviera, in equally close study of Bac's "magical gardens" of the Mediterranean and Spanish schools.

Barragan established himself in Mexico City in 1936, built a few homes and, revealing a shrewd business sense that no doubt also reflects his training as a youth, became involved in real-estate operations. He had constructed several gardens on the edge of the Pedregal — the Stony Place which he was to transform — and he sought, and found, financial and administrative partners with whom, in 1945, he acquired 750 acres of the rock whose possibilities now fascinated him. By 1948, he was able to form a company to develop the Pedregal as a residential area. He was to forsake the rigid controls he established over the design of houses and gardens, and he has "lived to lament the appearance of ostentatious architecture which detracts from the natural and developed beauty" of the region, but the Pedregal venture brought him fame and some wealth.

In succeeding years, Barragan landscaped Satellite City, on the outskirts of the capital; planned new tourist and residential areas on the Pacific coast, north of Manzanillo; and developed, on land crisscrossed by tree-lined roads and riders' paths that once comprised a *hacienda,* the Las Arboleadas residential zone that centers upon the La Hacienda Golf Club a few miles to the north of Mexico City.

To all these projects — and to others, ranging from reforestation to the construction of the famed *El Bebedero* and *El Campanario* plazas and the development of another new residential area, *Los Clubes* — Barragan has brought his unerring ability to recognize creativity and to harness it successfully with other creative talent. He whose work in architecture has been dedicated so largely to the protection of privacy now is trying to apply that doctrine to the planning of a self-contained city, *Ciudad Cumbres* — The Hill City — in which 100,000 people will live. Before the first plans were drawn, he traveled with the architect Juan Sordo Madaleno in Italy, France, Britain, Sweden and Denmark, studying the newest urban housing.

"In the face of the explosion of population, the problem of how to achieve harmony between large numbers of people and their surroundings, how to bring the beauty and serenity of parks and gardens into a multitude of homes, was bound to crop up sooner or later," he comments.

*Toda Arquitectura que
no exprese serenidad
no cumple con su
misión espiritual. Por
eso ha sido un error
substituir el abrigo
de los muros por la
+ intemperie de los
ventanales.*

Luis Barragán

"All architecture which does not express serenity fails in its spiritual mission. Thus it has been a mistake to abandon the shelter of walls for the inclemency of large areas of glass."

The Pedregal Gardens

El Pedregal — The Stony Place — is a frozen sea of volcanic rock, spread over an area of fifteen square miles. Toltecs and Aztecs quarried its rock for their cities, but through the centuries of Spanish rule it remained a desolate haunt of snakes, scorpions and coyotes.

Luis Barragan first became captivated by the Pedregal when he introduced a few fragments of the lava into his garden. Later, when he began the monumental task of landscaping and developing the Pedregal Gardens, he built a showpiece garden, using only the cacti, rock flowers, pepper trees and gnarled *palo bobo* (crazy tree) native to the region. The cultivation of grass lawns, which contrast vividly with the surrounding, multi-hued rock, presented no great problem. Rock projections were removed and used to build walls. Lawns grew quickly atop a layer of one foot of soil spread on the flat areas, and they drained most satisfactorily, water finding outlets through cracks in the rocks.

The Stony Place is by no means barren. Earth, formed by dust laid down by the rains during many hundreds of years, fills the cracks and minute basins of the porous rock. The rock also retains the heat of the sun, and radiates it. Thus many Pedregal walls have become vertical gardens in which moss, ferns and flowers flourish.

Originally, Pedregal residents conformed to a stiff zoning code. It is fitting that the first residential development in Mexico City to have required all houses to be of contemporary design should be situated on lava beds formed about 5000 years ago. Barragan adds: "It would be meaningless to restrict building designs for a residential development without also restricting landscaping. An excellent house can be degraded by a garden — or by a neighbor's garden."

Original and spectacular are the entrances to the Pedregal Gardens, once worthless land that was painstakingly transformed into an exclusive residential zone.

Pedregal lava, ranging in hue from reddish browns to grays, purples and black, provides exactly the starkly beautiful setting that Barragan sought for the modern homes he wanted to design.

Everyday life is becoming much too public, Luis Barragan protests. Radio, TV, the telephone, all invade privacy. Gardens therefore should be enclosed, not open to the public gaze.

"Open gardens are passed at fifty miles an hour, and scarcely are they glimpsed by the travelers. Nor are they ever used as gardens should be used, as living rooms, places to sit, to eat; meeting places for the people who live in the house."

"When can people meditate, living so much in public as they do? The public way of life actively prevents one from finding the peace, the serenity, that should be experienced every day."

"The construction and enjoyment of a garden accustoms people to beauty, to its instinctive use, even to its accomplishment."

The late Gerardo Murillo, better known as Dr. Atl, became world-famous for his paintings of Mexico's volcanos, mountains and upland valleys. He was also intrigued by the Pedregal, and when Barragan started to open it up the already venerable artist camped out in a rudimentary shelter among the rocks for some weeks, sketching the while. Three of the dozen drawings he presented to Barragan, hitherto unpublished, illustrate the dramatic nature of the wilderness that was to be made to flower, and the first roadway to be driven into the wasteland.

Fountain Los Clubes

Water plashes, murmurs — never roars — in the innumerable fountains, large or small, which Luis Barragan has fashioned.

As a decorator of exterior space, Barragan possibly is without peer. This, his latest fountain, stands in open country at *Los Clubes* (The Clubs) near Mexico City.

The high, massive, roughcast outer walls are magenta in color; the structure of the fountain is rust brown; the walks are of crushed yellow rock. Deep under the fall, the water shallows to an irridescent mirror as it moves outward over the purple-black cobblestones that line the basin, to gurgle down through cunningly contrived escapes.

The combination of colors sounds almost theatrical, but it happens that the perfectly proportioned structure conforms to, and reflects, its builder's impeccably good taste.

Los Amantes (The Lovers), as the two figures have been named, are in fact ancient, pitted wooden drinking troughs. The design of the fountain itself is, of course, that of a trough. Riders from nearby clubs bring their horses here to drink, or to let them plunge and roll under the sunshot water fall.

Los Amantes (The Lovers)

Barragan's Home

Luis Barragan's home, its blind walls edging a winding, unpretentious street in the Tacubaya neighborhood of Mexico City, is house and garden, the two inextricably entwined. The garden's formal, clipped lawn has been permitted to grow wild and tangled. Its serenity pervades the living rooms through windows set flush into ceiling, floor and walls. A pink brick, uncovered terrace is the favored dining room. Food is spread for the birds, so that the garden is alive with their soft song.

Barragan constructed his home to satisfy his personal taste, and in doing so established a new relationship between primary and rustic, but modern, materials and the type of architecture that is exemplified by the ranches and convents of parts of his home State, Jalisco, but especially by those of the State of Michoacan.

He used a reinforced concrete frame and concrete block, and commercial pine beams. High, plain outer walls have no window openings: indeed, all the more important rooms face inward to the garden. Thick, white inner walls, on the ground floor, rise only seven feet, far short of the ceilings, so that the rooms flow one into another and doors are conspicuous by their absence. The large wall surfaces reflect varying luminosity, which in turn creates a comfortable, intimate atmosphere.

"Architects are forgetting the need of human beings for half-light, the sort of light that imposes a sense of tranquillity, in their living rooms as well as in their bedrooms," Barragan observes. "About half the glass that is used in so many buildings — homes as well as offices — would have to be removed in order to obtain the quality of light that enables one to live and work in a more concentrated manner, and more graciously. We should try to recover mental and spiritual ease and to alleviate anxiety, the salient characteristic of these agitated times, and the pleasures of thinking, working, conversing are heightened by the absence of glaring, distracting light.

"Year by year, the height of ceilings diminishes and man, subconsciously, becomes the more depressed. Mark you, I admire LeCorbusier's work enormously, but the concept of building machines for living belittles the human being as well as detracting from, belittling, architecture. I fear that in our anthill structures, human personality is cribbed, confined, reduced to the lowest common denominator."

Luis Barragan is fond of paraphrasing a friend, a European critic, with whom he is in complete accord. "Before the machine age, even in the middle of the cities, Nature was everybody's trusted companion, partner of the baker, the butcher, blacksmith, carpenter," he comments. "Nowadays, the situation is reversed. Man does not meet with Nature, even when he leaves the city to commune with her. Enclosed in his shiny automobile, his spirit stamped with the mark of the world whence the automobile emerged, he is, within Nature, a foreign body. A billboard is sufficient to stifle the voice of Nature. Nature becomes a scrap of Nature, and man, a scrap of man. The intended dialogue between man and Nature becomes a hysterical, monotonous human monologue."

The beauty and ingenuity of this much-photographed
wooden staircase were more apparent
when the lower room still was unfurnished.

Barragan seems to have an aversion to the small, the fragile, the mediocre. Certainly his work is all to the contrary. Spaces and massive, roughly finished walls alike have great strength.

Tlalpam

Over a period of some six years, Luis Barragan, a devout Catholic, designed and built a convent in Tlalpam, a bosky suburb of Mexico City. When it was completed to his satisfaction, he gave it to the *Capuchinas Sacramentarias del Purissimo Corazon de María,* one of the most cloistered orders of his Church. The sisters rarely leave the convent.

Chapel, garden and house represent the best of Barragan: architectural strength of space; the handling of light as a sculptured medium; the use of few but rich tactile materials; infallibility in the choice of color. The simplicity and utter serenity of the chapel somehow defy explanation by a summing-up of its material parts.

The convent is a place of great beauty, achieved in a spirit of recognizably Franciscan austerity.

FELIX CANDELA

Felix Candela is a member of half a dozen professional organizations, and Honorary Member of the Colombian Society of Architects; the Venezuelan Society of Architects; the International Association for Shell Structure; the American Institute of Architects; the Royal Society of British Architects and the Church Architectural Guild of America.

He has been awarded the Gold Medal of the Institution of Structural Engineers of Great Britain (1961); the Auguste Perret Prize of the International Union of Architects (1961); the Charles Elliot Norton Professorship of Poetry, Harvard University, (1961-62); the Golden Seal of the Society of Mexican Architects (1963); a Doctorate in Fine Arts, Honoris Causa, University of New Mexico (1964) ; and the Alfred E. Lindau Award, American Concrete Institute (1965). In 1966, Sr. Candela is Visiting Professor, University of Virginia.

"HE was a master even as a student, a prodigy in class who helped his fellows generously, but in a spirit of pure comradeship, unostentatiously," recalled the magazine *Architecture,* of Madrid, some five years ago. Publication of columns of praise of Felix Candela, written by students, aging professors and his own contemporaries, coincided with that of his measured refusal to lecture in Madrid, the city of his birth. A stubborn, articulate Republican, he refuses to set foot in Franco's Spain.

Felix Candela Outeriño was born in January, 1910. His mother's family was of Galician and Basque descent, his father's, from the Province of Alicante.

It was during his first year at the Higher School of Architecture that he revealed a natural talent for geometry. During his third year, he studied the resistance of material under Luis Vegas, and went on to grapple with the Theory of Elasticity. His interest in laminar structures dates from that period. He still is fascinated by the problem of how a structure can be designed so as to prevent its collapse. Photographs of shell construction were being published in some European magazines, and Torroja was building the Fronton Recoletos in the Spanish capital. Candela felt intuitively that the key to understanding structures was to be found in mathematics, and he began to compile a bibliography of material on shells, translating as best he could from French, German and English.

All his life, Candela has believed in what he describes as "balanced development" — in physical exercise that preferably should include some element of risk, coupled with intense mental activity. He was the amateur skiing champion of Spain in 1932, a mountain climber, pole vaulter, hurdler and Rugby football player. Ideas might very well be digested — not dissipated — on a squash court, to emerge later only apparently as a product of the subconscious.

A year after his graduation in 1935, Candela was awarded a scholarship to study, in Germany, the use of concrete. Letters of introduction to the shell specialists Dischinger and Finsterwalter were in his pocket when, on the eve of his intended departure, the Civil War began. He enlisted in the government forces enthusiastically, and "learned from the war much more than the wise German professors could have taught me." In 1939, he crossed the border into France, together with half a million other soldiers. There, on a Mediterranean beach fenced with barbed wire and guarded by Senegalese machine gunners, he spent four months before his name appeared on a list of refugees who were to go to Mexico. He arrived in Veracruz on June 13, 1939, the tattered uniform of a Captain of Engineers his only possession.

In Mexico City, Candela worked five months in the offices of a construction company, as a draftsman. He rode a bus down to Acapulco, to help an architect build sixteen bungalows at the El Papagayo hotel, and returned to the capital to enter the offices of the architect Jesus Marti. For the next four years, says Candela, "I learned and learned, picking up every scrap of knowledge that was available about the construction of shells, struggling to understand technical articles in French, German, English, even in Danish and Swedish."

Meanwhile, his brother Antonio, an engineer, had joined him from Europe. Together they built an apartment house and a hotel, conventional buildings that did nothing to assuage Felix' thirst for practical experiments in shell construction — a thirst that grew with the success of his laboratory experiments with foam concrete. Convinced that the form, not the mass, gives resistance, he became annoyed with engineers who turned down his projects "on the pretext that earthquakes and defective subsoils made them impracticable." But he both felt and knew that his conclusions were correct. He read more and more skeptically, and his approach to problems of building became more and more individual and unconventional.

His sense of frustration deepened until one day a friend quite casually invited him to try his hand at "one of those curious structures of yours." The building, a bowling alley, was spectacular in its day, successful and economical, and two more small shells were built in short order.

It so happened that the National University of Mexico wanted, at this time, to build a pavilion for the study of cosmic rays. To the dismay of the city's architects, the University blandly specified a roof just one centimeter thick. Candela accomplished an extraordinarily thin roof of one and one-half centimeters, and immediately was inundated with invitations to lecture.

He was already writing on shell structures. He had, indeed, in 1951, formulated "A New Philosophy of Structures" in which he cut himself loose from all conventional methods of calculation.

Public speaking proved to be an agonizing experience, but his lectures were nonetheless stimulating. He assaulted the Theory of Elasticity, architects in general and "mathematical engineers" in particular, objecting strongly to the indiscriminate application of the theory to structural analysis, especially as related to reinforced concrete design "because the behavior of this material is in total disagreement with elastic assumptions."

Goaded at one lecture, he invited his critics to provide him with a mathematical expression defining the form of the vaults filling the space between groins in a Gothic cathedral, and added, blithely: "Of course, no Gothic cathedral could be built today, since the most lax Building Department would declare it to be unsafe."

Shells multiplied, in a wider and wider profusion of forms, and by 1952 they were more numerous in Mexico than in any other country. The Candela brothers' construction company built warehouses, chapels, factories and a few houses: in one of these houses, which was to be raffled by a daily newspaper, they gleefully overheard an architect's comment that the designers obviously were smokers of marijuana. But the ubiquitous shells were not to be denied. Gently they floated into the provinces, into Cuba, Venezuela, Puerto Rico, Peru and, finally, into the western United States of America.

Sure of himself as by now he was, Candela nevertheless caught his second wind in 1954, when he presented two papers at a conference at the Massachusetts Institute of Technology. He read his first paper: "The Shell as a Space Encloser" in English and, since nobody had understood a word of it, the second, on "Warped Surfaces" was read for him while he wrote an accompaniment of formulae on a blackboard. Vigorously and critically questioned from the floor, he started to explain, "in my horrible English," that success generally is obtained by attention to details of the modeling of points of support, and does not necessarily have much to do with the general form of the shell. He paused, shrugged his shoulders, pointed to his formulae, and sat down.

"Having brought with me a fearful complex about the prestige of the place and the author-

ity of the experts gathered there, I found myself somewhat ahead of the experts and, incidentally, rid of the last remnant of doubt," he grins. "Also, since those days, I have learned to speak clearly, but using a deliberately limited English vocabulary. Most people seem enchanted to be able to discuss fairly complicated matters in elementary terms."

He returned to Mexico City to construct the La Virgen Milagrosa church which, upon completion, was described by various enthusiasts as "a highly individualistic architectural statement" . . . "an engineering ploy of great sophistication" . . . "a building that could not have been executed or even conceived by any other contemporary architect."

Candela recalls only the agonizing doubts the priests of the parish suffered during the period of construction. "Architects don't like it," he admits, "but then, it wasn't built for them. Too much music is written for musicians, too many pictures are painted for painters. Nobody remembers the people, and the people love this church."

Some at first thought that for economic and climatic reasons, shell construction would prove to be practical only in a country such as Mexico. They were mistaken to the extent that Candela now is associated with a group of architects in New York City.

"Relatively, labor costs are no higher than in Mexico," he comments. "Building regulations are different — all that weight of snow — but the climate in the U.S. is the same as in Northern Europe. I did not invent these concrete roofs, but they are practical, economical, and becoming widely used in Latin America. Perhaps we will be able to build bigger spans in the United States, even if we stay within the tradition of U.S. architecture for the moment. This new venture is a challenge. It gives me the same sense of exhilaration that I first experienced as a mountain climber."

Candela has roofed some 4,000,000 square feet with umbrellas, in the capital of Mexico alone. This photograph, taken just after the forms had been removed at the Cabero warehouse in the industrial zone of Vallejo in 1957, reveals the beauty of the umbrella form. In the finished building the floor, walls and roof are of the same subdued gray, and the white columns emphasize the sense of unified space.

Signpost at the entrance to a residential complex bordering Lake Tequesquitengo, Morelos.
Architects: Guillermo Rosell and Manuel Larrosa.

CANDELABRIA

"It is always simple to explain the way you have done things, after you have accomplished them. But in most cases, such explanations are completely false because one does not know exactly when — or even how — one reached a certain point in one's thinking. It is not the conscious mind that surmounts a problem, step by step. The logical process always is understood after the fact, and often most imperfectly."

"One of the most interesting qualities of human intelligence is its ability to clarify a theme in order to simplify it. A problem must first be stripped of everything that is unnecessary and superfluous. Once the essence is bared, the rest is easy. Everything is so simple when once you know it that you are really angry for not having seen it all at first glance, instead of having had to endure the painful process of thinking. I knew, for instance, that the free edge was a practical idea, long before I understood intellectually how it worked. I don't know if others are conscious of the moment at which a certain phenomenon occurs, but it always has amused me to observe that, all of a sudden, one is doing things that were impossible to do. The sensation is like that of an athlete who, at a given moment, and after a long period of training, feels himself in form."

"Functionalism is a philosophical architectural theory. There is no spectacle more sad than that offered by a triumphant revolution whose ideological content, political and philosophical program, does not withstand the test of reality. Functionalism was the flag, the literary justification, of a revolution whose immediate objective was simply the overthrow of historical styles. It very quickly became boring."

"I spend a lot of time explaining what I cannot do, or why I cannot do what is asked of me. My principal task is to simplify, to convince people that success does not depend upon building extravagant forms but only, on the contrary, upon making simple ones, and studying the details with care and with love. This is the norm that should apply to any architectural work.

"Structural design has much more to do with art than with science, being based on the investigations of scientists. Certainly I have never been attracted to pure mathematics, because of my abominable memory. I have only tried to develop visual intelligence and some talent for analytical geometry and trigonometry."

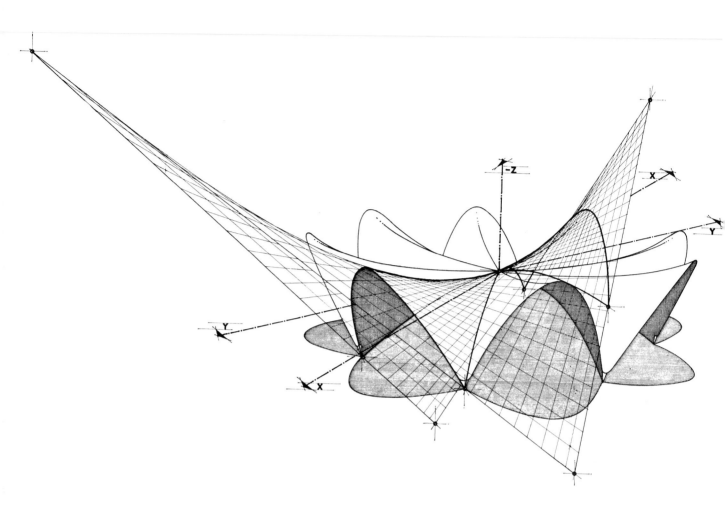

If concrete space enclosers one day become lighter than the wind, architects and builders will have to revise their manuals and regulations drastically. Candela's dedication to calculating them seems to stem from his determination to force mathematics to bow to an idea. Sensing that the "free edge," admirably achieved in the "Los Manantiales" restaurant at Xochimilco, Mexico City, was feasible, his almost interminable investigation had a dual goal. Architect: Joaquin Alvarez Ordoñez.

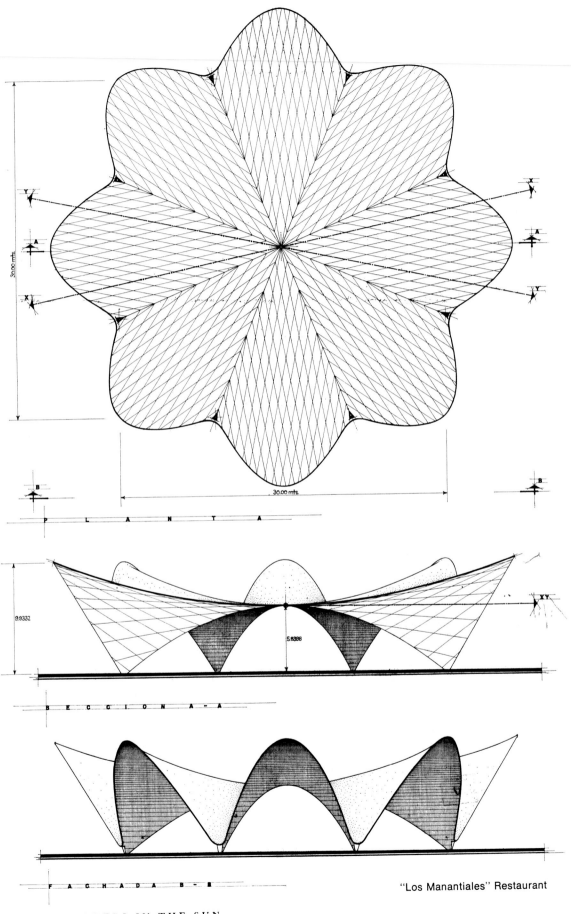

PLANTA

3000 mts.

30.00 mts.

9.9332

5.8388

SECCION A-A

FACHADA B-B

"Los Manantiales" Restaurant

La Jacaranda nightclub, Hotel El Presidente, Acapulco. Architect: Juan Sordo Madaleno.

"It is not the specific job of the architect to invent structures, but the architect must have a clear idea of the play of forces in a building. There is no way to acquire structural intuition, the ability to design and calculate buildings visually, except by doing innumerable calculations — routine and boring, perhaps — but which, little by little, yield this sixth or seventh sense without which it is difficult to be a builder."

A trio of groined vaults at the Bacardi plant north of Mexico City measure 100 square feet each. Exterior and interior of the Bacardi de Mexico bottling plant, Km. 34, Carretera México — Queretaro. Architects: Saenz-Cancio-Martin-Alvarez & Gutierrez.

Sales office, Guadalajara. Architect: Alfredo Terrazas de la Peña.

"Organization should not be confused with progress. Progressive countries are supposed to be the best organized, but ants and birds long ago achieved operative perfection, and they haven't progressed at all in millions of years. Organization is conservative, static.

"Who can agree on what constitutes architecture or, even less, on what is the mission of the architect? The fashionable concept, at the moment, is that of the architect as a leader in the constructive process, the boss of a group of specialists, charged with the divine mission of planning a country, at least, if not the whole world, and of resolving a major social problem of our times.

"This heroic portrait of the architect as a savior of humanity naturally has been accepted, enthusiastically, and has demoralized our students. If they are to be directors, why should they waste their time in learning to draw when draftsmen are available? Why learn to understand the function of a beam, when mathematicians can accept the responsibility? Why plan hydraulic installations, which is the job of mechanical engineers?

"It is an illusion to believe that a student can be transformed into an architect in four or five years. The formation of any professional takes a lifetime."

Entrance structure, Lederle Laboratories, Calzada de Tlalpam, Mexico City. Architect: Alejandro Prieto.

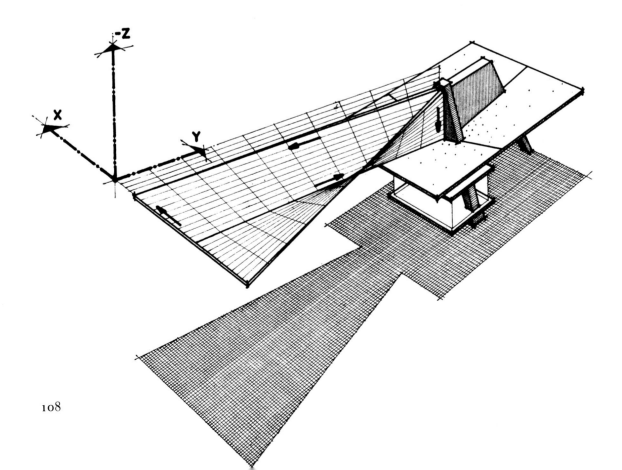

"Recently, everybody has been trying to invent extraordinary structures. The irresponsible and frivolous architects who are engaged in this dangerous game forget — if they ever knew it — that the creative act never results from easy inspiration, but as an often tardy consequence of long, hard work, many years of dedication, of insistence on the theme.

"Brazilia? A pseudo-city built with scandalous, publicity-seeking zeal. Brazilia! The TWA terminal at the New York City airport! The results of the more important international competitions must fill the juries and the profession as a whole with shame! Who has dared to denounce the Sydney Opera House, or to lament the abject failure of the San Sebastian competition? Paris is full of exhibitions of mad, tasteless, impractical projects for cities of the future, and they are photographed, reproduced and praised, whilst nobody pauses to think of the change of scale, the impossibility of such gigantic proportions. A flea can jump many times its height. An elephant cannot get off the ground. The consciousness of physical limitations must be inculcated. Problems must be approached in a spirit of simplicity and humility."

"The Candela Shell" decorates the grounds of an annual Flower Fair in Oslo.

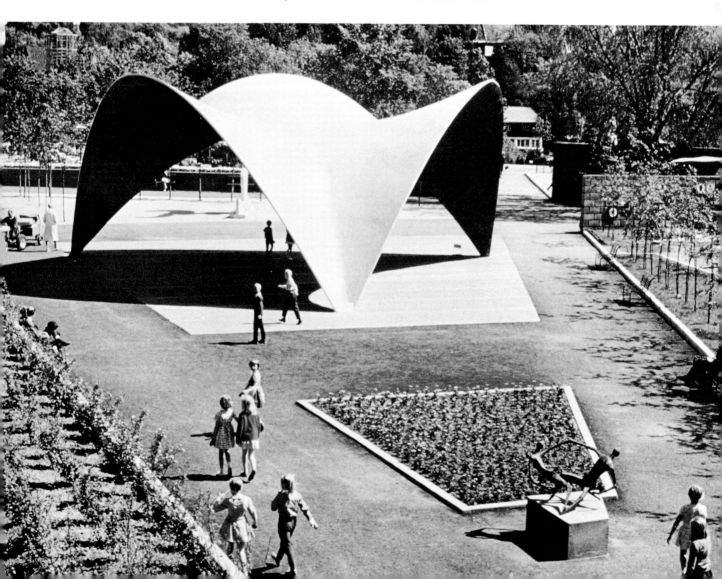

Mexico City Stock Exchange. Architects: Enrique de la Mora and Fernando Lopez Carmona. Early in 1954 the architects De la Mora and Lopez Carmona designed a doubly curved vault to roof the main hall of the new Exchange. Their idea seemed to be untenable until they discussed it with Candela, who made the shell from the intersection of two paraboloids. It stands on the third floor of an eight-story building.

Most of Candela's shells are a nominal 1.5 inches thick. The concrete need only be thick enough to insulate the steel it embodies, and the reinforcing mesh need do little more than bind the concrete.

Any engineer might regard edge beams or stiffening ribs as nothing more than elements discharging a necessary function, but to Candela they obviously represent challenge. If they can be discarded, the idea of the shell is realized.

Nothing more could be removed from Candela's free-edge masterpieces. There is no compromise to their thinness. No props, ribs or stabilizers support them. Their strength therefore must reside in their shape.

Candelabria

"The essence of architecture resides in the absence of originality. Every sudden change in the habitual language invites disaster. The language of architecture, one of abstract symbols, nevertheless is divided as between style and character. Character is the formal symbolism that differentiates some buildings from others.

"There must exist certain individuals who dedicate their time to the investigation of structure, to the search for new, resistant, forms. I refer to the qualitative, formalist type of investigation. Theory alone is not sufficient: it must be accompanied by progressive realization, and by essays on a natural scale. It might happen, in the course of such work, and almost by accident, that certain forms are discovered which might develop into types capable of widening the repertoire of architecture. Although the investigation might, at the beginning, have no architectonic pretensions, its results could enrich architecture.

"The conditions these structural types must observe are: (a) economy, in terms of the consumption of materials and the ease of construction; (b) calculation that is relatively simple, not the exclusive knowledge of a few specialists; (c) form that is sufficiently flexible to permit adaptation to various uses.

"My greatest satisfaction is not in having achieved certain spectacular structures, even though I enjoy doing them, but in having helped in a small way to solve the problem of covering habitable spaces economically: in having shown that the construction of umbrella shells, for instance, is not an extraordinary hazard that immortalizes their builders, but a simple and flexible constructive procedure. It has become of common usage in many countries, and it is available to architects in their specific task of achieving beauty by simple methods."

Candela's Churches

"If the church is a guardian of morals, we might consider the virtues of functionalism — integrity, honesty, humility, even poverty — the most desirable qualities of a religious building.

"But there have been other epochs in which an idealistic philosophy was the basis of human civilization, and spiritual wellbeing was considered to be more important than the possession of material goods. Religion should be the last to retreat from such idealistic concepts. All efforts to rationalize religion are, indeed, contrary to the ultimate spiritual objective of religion itself, so even the design of a religious building might be somewhat irrational, governed more by emotional feelings than by strict, conventional logic."

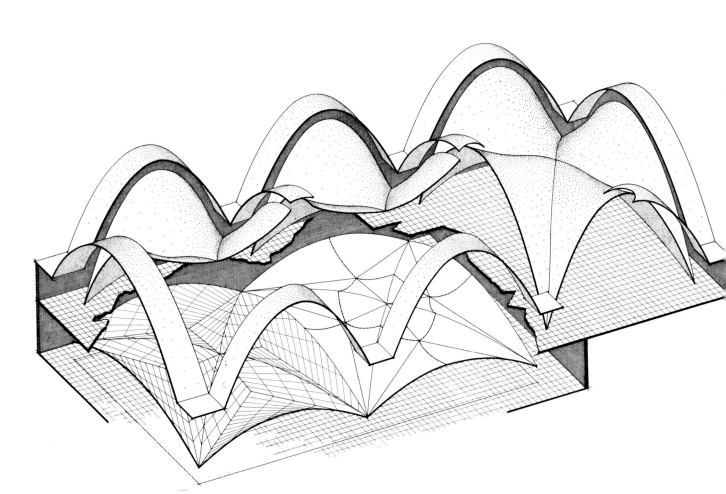

La Iglesia San Antonio de las Huertas (St. Anthony of the Orchards Church), Mexico City.
Architects: Enrique de la Mora and Fernando Lopez Carmona.

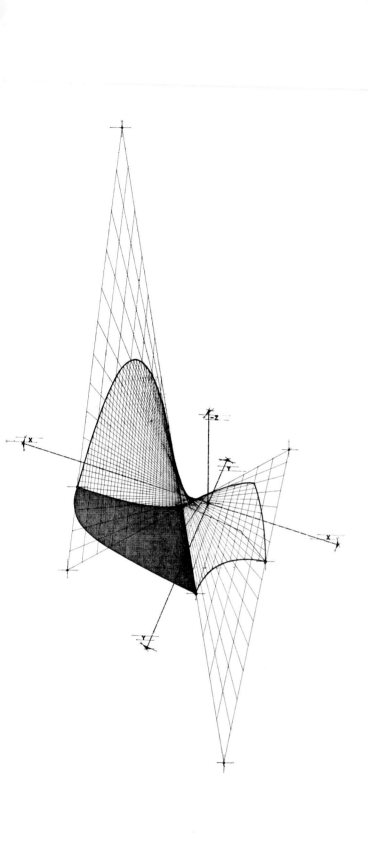

Chapel at Lomas de Cuernavaca, Morelos. Architects: Guillermo Rosell and Manuel Larrosa. The chapel, built on the crest of a lonely hill, catches the eye from many parts of the sweeping valley of Cuernavaca or from the mountain road ten miles to the north. The congregation sits on tiers under the greater roof, which sinks only to rise again and reveal the broad valley and the snowy crests of Popocatapetl and Ixtaccihuatl.

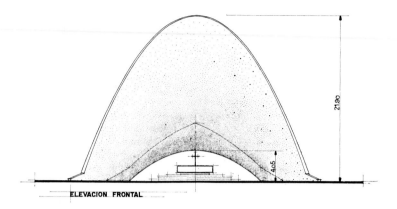

ELEVACION FRONTAL

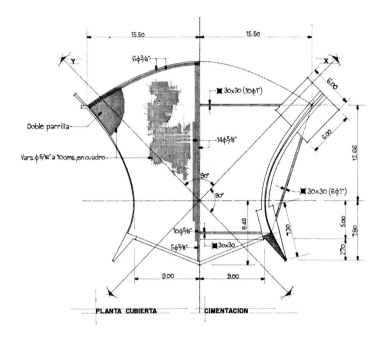

6φ3/4"

Doble parrilla

Vars.φ5/16"a 10cms,en cuadro

30x30 (10φ1")

14φ5/8"

90°

90°

30x30 (6φ1")

10φ5/8"

5φ5/8"

30x30

PLANTA CUBIERTA   CIMENTACION

Chapel at Lomas de Cuernavaca, Morelos.

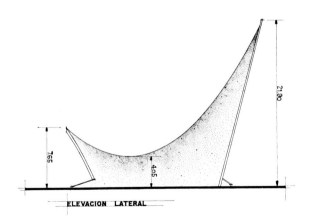

ELEVACION LATERAL

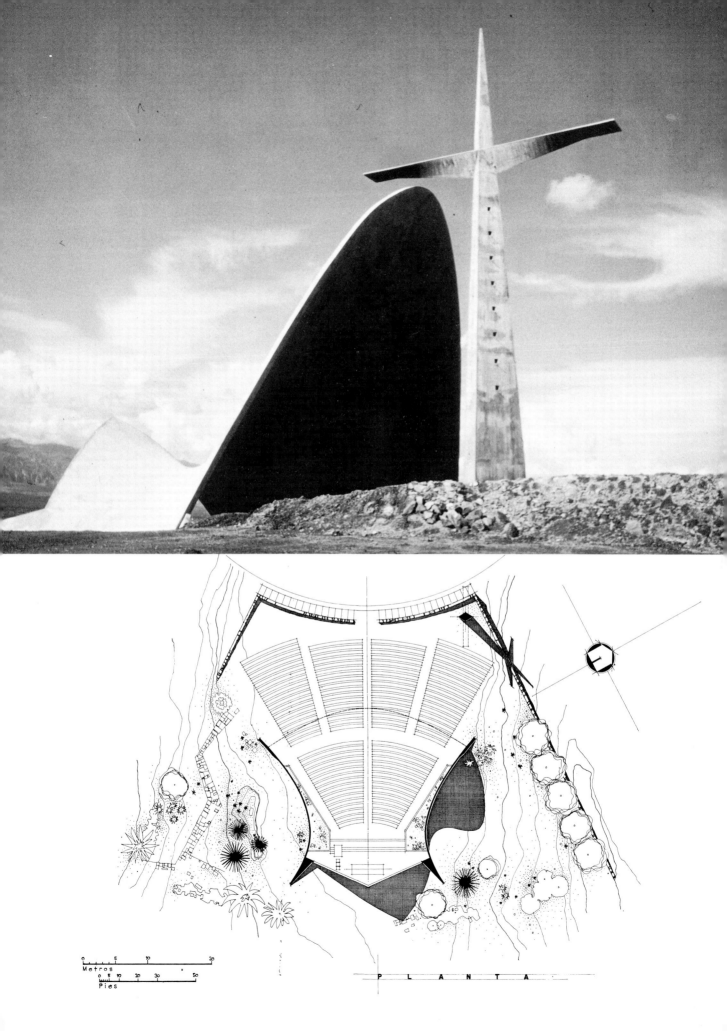

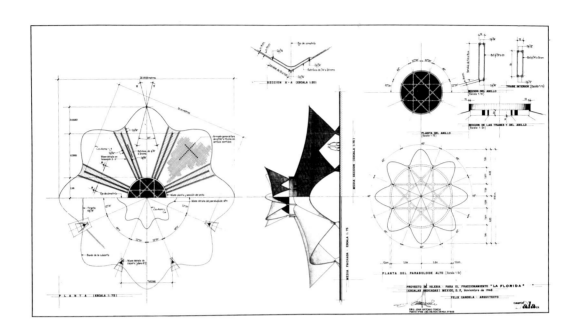

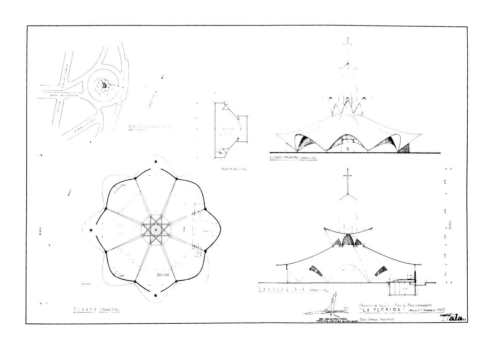

La Florida Church, Satellite City, State of Mexico

"The highest peaks of religious feeling were attained by mystics who, according to modern standards, were by no means reasonable people. They sought direct knowledge of absolute truth, a knowledge that cannot be reached by a logical or rational process of thought, but by the intervention of the subconscious after a long and painful period of hard work. This is the process which brings about artistic creation and is the basis of all inventions. The subconscious is much more reliable than usually is thought, as artists and saints have known for centuries.

The winged silhouette of the San José Obrero (St. Joseph the Worker) Church leaps against the sky on the outskirts of the northern industrial city of Monterrey. Each wing is a hypar bent back upon itself. The photograph reveals both the seeming fragility of the shell roof and the complexity of the work of the carpenters, who, having added the last, highest crosspiece, adorned it with their own primitive Cross. Architect: Enrique de la Mora.

Iglesia de San Pedro Martir (Church of St. Peter the Martyr), Mexico City. Architects: Gustavo and Hugo Escudero.

"The irrational or intuitive methods of design might not be so illogical, after all. They depend on the capricious and sporadic functioning of the subconscious, but, as a geometrician, I am inclined to believe them to be the only way really to design anything.

"Not that I am an artist, or a saint, or a religious man. I am not even an architect. I do not make architecture. I do not work as an architect. I am a contractor."

La Iglesia de la Virgen Milagrosa (The Church of Our Miraculous Lady), Mexico City.

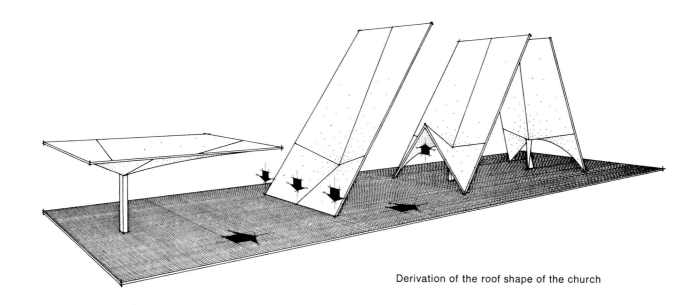

Derivation of the roof shape of the church

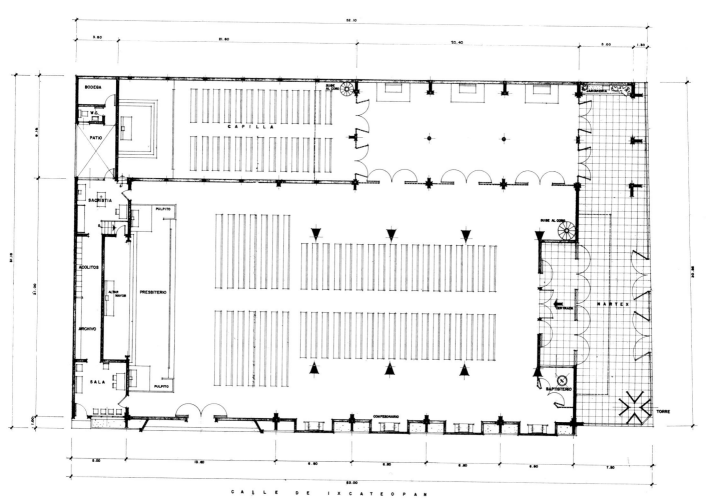

PLANTA A ESCALA I:100.

Plan of La Virgen Milagrosa Church

La Iglesia de la Virgen Milagrosa

La Iglesia de la Virgen Milagrosa

La Iglesia de la Virgen Milagrosa

In midsummer 1966 the Santa Monica Church in Mexico City, designed by Fernando Lopez Carmona, was in use — completed so far as Candela was concerned: lacking only architectural details, interior decoration and the demolition of a temporary workshop and entrance. Meanwhile the Candela roof loomed large above a new residential area of the city.

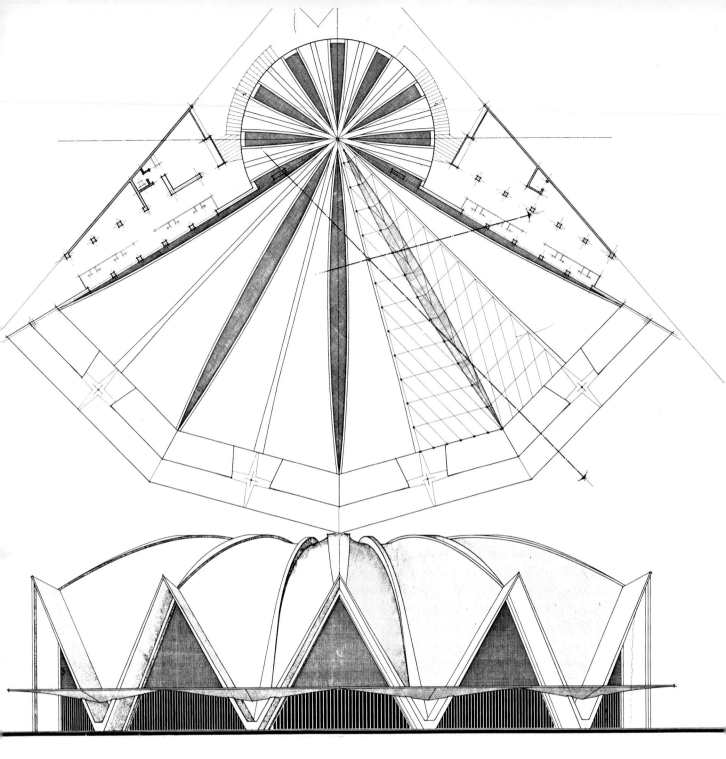

Santa Monica Church in Mexico City

mathias Goeritz

MATHIAS GOERITZ

"MATHIAS GOERITZ is a mere fake, without the least talent or preparation for the exercise of an art in which he poses as a professional." The joint authors of this public statement, the painters Diego Rivera and David Alfaro Siqueiros, were at the height of their fame and authority. Yet the subject of their scorn, his head bloodied but unbowed, impassively continued to paint, to sculpt, to teach architecture, to build a controversial, experimental building. Michel Seuphor rose to defend him as "among the best of all the sculptors." Claudio Cevallos praised him as "a man of the Renaissance, in whom thousands of young artists sense the mysticism of the truly great artist."

Years later, in 1963, Frederick Kissler rejoiced in Mathias as "a man who can do anything. He really CAN and he really DOES: a painting, a chair, a sculpture, stained-glass windows, poems illustrated with typewritten types, dance poems constructed in steel — carving wood, casting Christ in bronze. Mathias erects modern obelisks, skyscraping pylons, which scream to heaven and denounce the earth.

"Sometimes he uses nails instead of paint, the heads of nails that march, march, obeying his commands, in strict formations, steel helmets of a peace army.

"He is a 'gamuteur,' an artist who can run any gamut of the plastic arts, sculpting in the round, in iron, wood or concrete, or flattening a painter's panel with line and color. With his pylons and towers he fingers architecture, which I am sure he is most capable of bursting into — a universal artist, sweeping the earth while depositing the work of his labors and of his mind everywhere, signals to a world en route to nowhere. Thus he leads us away from disaster."

Drawn by his work and his teaching into controversy, in Mexico, in the U.S.A., in Europe, Mathias relishes the fact that much of his work in architecture is anonymous. Disinterested service is the ideal to be sought. The artist of the next century will, he hopes, be anonymous, as in the Middle Ages.

At times, he cannot contain his wrath. In London, in 1965, he exploded: "Many of us are fed up with the pretentious imposition of 'logic' and 'reason' and 'functionalism'; with the decorative calculation and of course with all the chaotic pornography of individualism, the glory of the day, the fashion of the moment; with vanity, cruelty, violence and ambition; with the bluff and the artistic jest, the conscious and subconscious egotism; with all the inflated concepts, the boring propaganda of the isms, figurative or abstract.

"As for me, I feel the need to abandon the

worship of the ego, and to deflate 'art.' I am convinced that esthetic beauty in our times is more vigorous when the so-called artist hardly intervenes.

"Deeply conscious as I am of my own impotence, I do not see any choice but to believe, without asking in what. All the established values must be rectified. Let us try to turn man's work into a plastic prayer.

"Do you understand me, dear friend?" he enquired of his interviewer. "Well, don't worry: neither, perhaps, do I."

A complex personality indeed, a typical modern intellectual engaged in a relentless search for ethical and esthetic values to satisfy him and to offer to his fellow men.

"Am I an architect?" he asks. "Well, I have been teaching architecture for seventeen years in Mexico. I am a member of the Faculty of the School of Architecture of the National University. I am a collaborator, an artistic counselor to prominent architects of two generations. I have no office, no draftsmen, no designers. I make my own drawings, my own models, realize my own ideas.

"Perhaps I am not an architect," he frowns. "The only time I was able to construct a whole building to my own taste, my own design, was in 1952, when a friend, Daniel Mont, invited me to build 'absolutely anything you wish' on a relatively small piece of land in the center of Mexico City."

That building, El Eco, caused furious discussion, particularly among painters, sculptors and architects of various nationalities.

Being primarily a sculptor and painter, Goeritz had never taken any particular note of the logical form of a building. He had always been aware of the profound impression caused by the great works that contain within themselves all the arts. It is difficult for him to decide where the elements of architecture, sculpture, painting, or even poetry, begin or end in, for instance, a Gothic cathedral.

So he decided that El Eco would be an example of what he chose to call Emotional Architecture, and that its function would be that of an Experimental Museum. Art in general, and architecture, he proclaimed, "is a reflection of the spiritual state of man in his time. But much modern architecture is too individual, too intellectual, too rational.

Twentieth-century man feels crushed by so much functionalism, so much logic in contemporary architecture. Nobody wants to face up to the fact that man — creative or not — aspires to something more than a pretty, agreeable or merely adequate dwelling place. He asks of architecture, its media, its materials, its practitioners, some spiritual inspiration: an emotion, such as he received from the architecture of the pyramids — especially those of Mexico — the Greek temples, the Romanesque or Gothic cathedrals, even the Baroque castles. Only if he receives some such emotion can man again come to consider architecture as an art.

"Our times are full of deep spiritual unrest. The Experimental Museum sought nothing more than to express it, and to cause the greatest possible emotional impact."

El Eco was built in 1952-53. An impression of depth was obtained through walls that varied in height between twenty and thirty-six feet. There was hardly a ninety-degree angle visible. Corridors narrowed almost to a point. Integration was not planned. The architectural space had to be understood as a large sculptured element, though with none of Gaudi's romanticism or of empty German or Italian neo-classicism.

"The building was an effort to reawaken, within modern architecture, the psychic emotions that are latent in man. It tried to express the free will to create, and to add spiritual content to the achievements of functionalism. I sought the asymmetry that is found in any human face, any living thing. There were no friendly curves. It was all done on the spot, without exact plans. Mason, painter, sculptor, architect were one person."

The echo became inaudible amid the uproar of controversy. It also became, after an initial success as a showplace for artists, a hall for religious meetings, a restaurant and a cabaret.

It seemed that this experiment in building influenced Goeritz' sculpture. "Volumes of monumental size interested me now. I dreamed of building an immense cathedral or pyramid." Four years later, in 1957, he had a chance to put something of this into practice, when the landscape of a Satellite City on the northern edge of the capital was being planned. "I thought of the San Gimignano towers, the skyscrapers of Manhattan, and designed five triangular towers, varying in color and, in height, from thirty-seven to fifty-seven meters. But their function was purely emotional. Most architects say they are nothing more than sculpture. They are right. But for me they were painting, sculpture, emotional architecture. I wanted to place tiny flutes on their corners, so that passers-by would hear strange songs played by the wind, and the towers would become music, too. For most people, these towers are merely an advertisement. For me, an absurd romantic in a century that lacks faith, they are a plastic prayer."

El Eco, meanwhile, had centered attention on its builder. In 1954, Goeritz was appointed to head the new Visual Education Workshop of the National School of Architecture of the University of Mexico. In 1956, the Ibero-American University asked him to organize a new Fine Arts School, which he directed for some five years.

Whence comes this unwitting disturber of academic peace? Werner Mathias Goeritz Brunner was born in Danzig in April, 1915, son of the city's Mayor, Ernst Goeritz, and Hedwig Brunner, the daughter of a painter.

Soon afterward, the family moved to Berlin, where Goeritz studied at the School of Arts and Crafts and obtained his Ph.D. in the History of Art. He traveled extensively in Europe in the Thirties, feeling himself "a stranger in my own country, where the dictatorship created an atmosphere of fear and anguish, and artists and intellectuals generally were damned as degenerates." When war came, he was working as an art historian in the National Galerie, but he contrived to travel to Tetuan, Morocco, in 1941. There, and later in Granada, Spain,

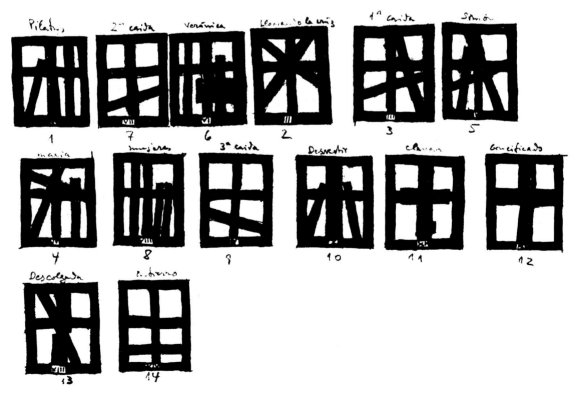

he lived by painting and teaching. In 1947, he won recognition in Madrid for a series of sculptures, "Variations on the theme of the Crucifixion," and in the following year founded the Altamira School of Art on the north coast of Spain.

In 1949 he accepted an invitation to join the Mexican architect Ignacio Diaz Morales, who had established a School of Architecture in Guadalajara. During his first two years in that Mexican provincial capital, he founded, or helped to found, four art galleries, and taught Visual Education at the State University. Two pieces of his sculpture, commissioned for the Casino de Guadalajara, were immediately removed, to mollify the outraged members. But one of the pieces was bought for the entrance to the Pedregal Gardens in Mexico City, and the other served as the model for a cement figure that stands at the door of the El Presidente Hotel, in Acapulco. Trying to integrate plastic expression with architecture, he worked in forged iron, made incrusted mural decorations and designed mosaics for walls and floors.

He has made, and not merely designed, some 200 stained-glass windows for the Cathedrals of Mexico City and Cuernavaca, and for various churches in the capital.

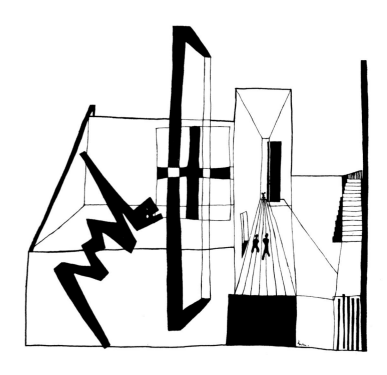

What has he contributed to architecture in Mexico? "Perhaps a touch of asymmetry," he ventures. "Also, perhaps, the introduction of more sculpture into building, and the deliberate use of exaggerated proportions. Why, even my cathedral windows are irregular in shape. I, in turn, always have been astounded — and probably influenced — by the magnificence and the proportions of the constructions at the archeological sites I have visited in many parts of Mexico."

El Eco, Experimental Museum, Mexico City.
Facade. 1952-53.
Photo: Marianne Goeritz.

140   El Eco. Entrance-corridor.
Photo: Armando Salas Portugal.

El Eco. Dancer Pilar Pellicer. Mural decoration (detail) designed by Henry Moore (1953).
Sculpture by Mathias Goeritz (1952).
Photo: Marianne Goeritz.

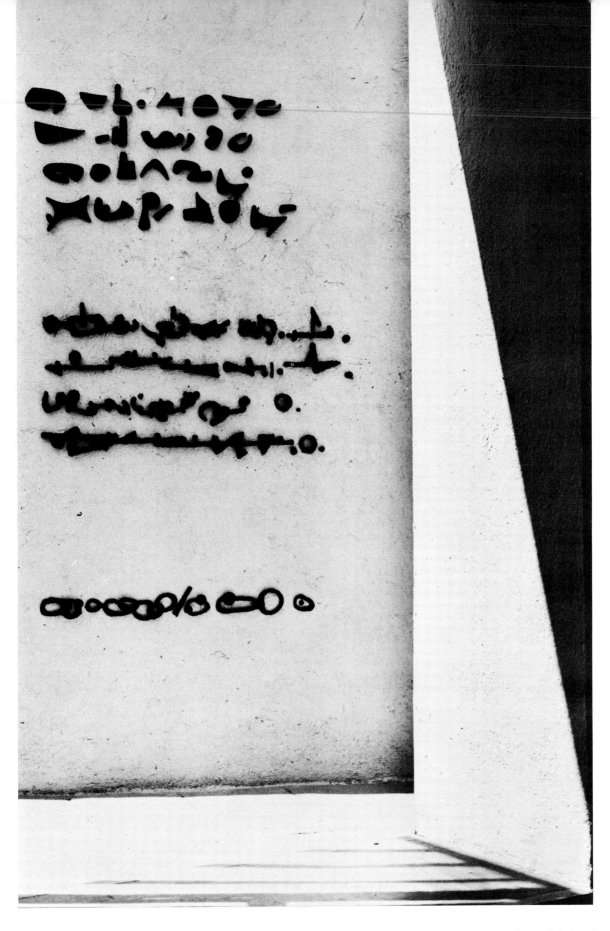

El Eco. "El Poema Plastico," by Mathias Goeritz: iron shapes on a yellow painted wall.
Photo: Marianne Goeritz.

El Eco. Freestanding yellow wall in the patio.
Photo: Marianne Goeritz.

El Eco. Three dancers of El Eco's Experimental Ballet, posed before an interchangeable iron sculpture by Goeritz which served as a setting for theater or ballet performances.
Photo: Marianne Goeritz.

El Eco. View of the patio.
Photo: Armando Salas Portugal.

Here and There: series "Emotional Architecture." Wood sculpture, polychromed. 1955. (Coll. T. Creighton, New York)
Photo: Marianne Goeritz.

The City of the Seven Towers: series "Emotional Architecture." Wood sculpture, poly-chromed. 1956.
Photo: Marianne Goeritz.

Realizations: series "Environment Sculpture." Painted wood. 1957-59. (Coll. J. Patrick Lannan Foundation, Palm Beach)

The Towers of Satellite City: Mexico City-Queretaro highway. 1957. Painted concrete. The tallest tower is 190 feet high. City planner of Ciudad Satelite: Mario Pani. Landscape architect: Luis Barragán.
Photo: Marianne Goeritz.

The Towers of Satellite City. A side view.
Photo: Marianne Goeritz.

The Towers of Satellite City. General View.
Photo: Tor Eigeland.

The Towers of Satellite City. Detail.
Photo: Marianne Goeritz.

The Towers of Satellite City. Details.
Photo: Marianne Goeritz.

The Towers of Satellite City. Detail.
Photo: Marianne Goeritz.

The Towers of Satellite City. Detail.
Photo: Marianne Goeritz.

The Yellow Bird. Painted concrete, fifty feet high. 1957. Entrance to Jardines del Bosque housing development, Guadalajara, Jalisco. In collaboration with Luis Barragán, architect. Photo: Horst Hartung.

Construction: series ''Emotional Architecture.'' Polychromed wood. 1957.
Photo: Marianne Goeritz.

Mexican Construction: series "Emotional Architecture." Polychromed wood and iron. 1959.

Emotional Construction: series "Emotional Architecture." Polychromed iron. 1959. (Coll. I. Clert, Paris.)

Emotional Construction. Exhibited in a public square in a working-class area of Mexico City.

Dome and nave stained-glass windows, Azcapotzalco Parochial Church, Mexico City. 1961-62.
Wrought iron. Architect for the reconstruction of the church: Ricardo de Robina.

← Iron railings at the Smith, Kline & French Laboratories, Mexico City. 1964. In collaboration
with Ricardo Legorreta, architect.
Photo: Kati Horna.

Road sign for VAM (Willys-Rambler) factory, Mexico City-Toluca highway. Painted concrete, ninety feet long. 1964. In collaboration with Carlos Mijares, architect.
Photo: Kati Horna.

Towers at the entrance of the Maguen-David Synagogue, Mexico City. 1964-65. In collaboration with David Serur, engineer, and Guillermo Hume, architect.
Photo: Kati Horna.

The Yellow Wall. Freestanding wall which creates the main square of the Unidad Adolfo Lopez Mateos housing development in the State of Mexico. Sixty feet high. 1964. In collaboration with the Instituto Nacional de la Vivienda.

Constructions: series "Do It Yourself" sculpture. Bronze. 1960. (Coll. Mrs. Herbert Morris, Philadelphia.)

The Towers of Automex. Symbols of the New Mexican automobile-manufacturing industry, near Toluca, State of Mexico. About 135 feet high. 1963-64. In collaboration with Ricardo Legorreta, architect.
Photo: Kati Horna.

The Towers of Automex.
Photo: Kati Horna.

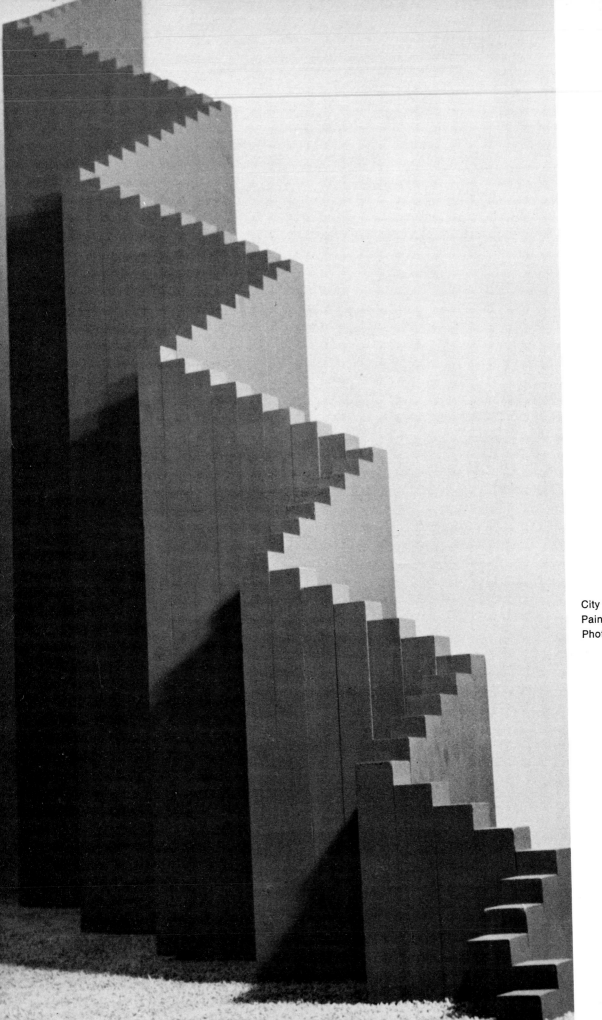

City project. "The Endless C
Painted wood. 1960.
Photo: Kati Horna.

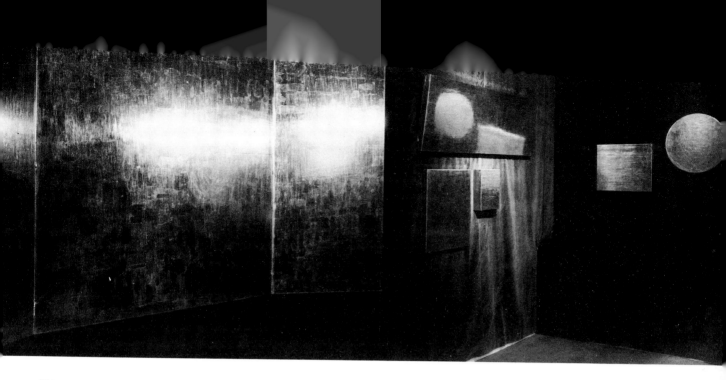

"Message." Golden environment sculpture, Carstairs Gallery, New York. 1960.
Photo: Rudolph Burckhardt.

"Messages." Gilded wood. 1960.
Photo: Rudolph Burckhardt.

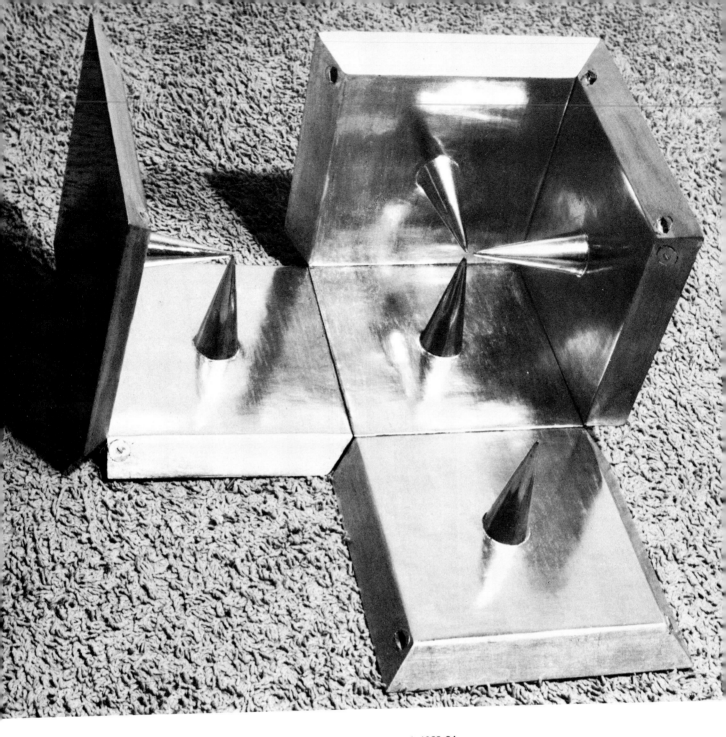

Cross in the Box. Project for a cathedral. Gilded wood. 1963-64.
Photo: Kati Horna.

Cross in the Box. Project for a cathedral. Gilded wood. 1963-64.
Photo: Kati Horna.

MARIO PANI

"Mankind must build, in the next thirty-five years, more homes than it has built in the past five thousand years!" Mario Pani throws up his hands in amazement. "How we have taken ourselves by surprise! How unprepared we were — and are!

"The population of Mexico did not even double during the nineteenth Century. In 1910, my father, with a number of other engineers, made plans to supply drinking water for six hundred thousand people who one day, they supposed, would live in Mexico City. Everybody said the plans were exaggerated, extravagant. But now, more than six millions live in the metropolitan area. Each year, the population increases by three hundred fifty thousand, and the rate of growth is increasing, too. Imagine! The index of the birth rate in Mexico is higher than in India, China, Indonesia. By the year 2000, we Mexicans will number one hundred twenty millions, with Mexico City all the time growing twice as fast as the rest of the country."

Pani moves forward in his chair, and continues, gravely: "On the eastern fringes of Mexico City, on and around the dry bed of Lake Texcoco, a million people somehow exist, without sanitation, without proper shelter." He taps his desk impatiently. "Another three hundred thousand people crouch in caves in the lava that is part of the Pedregal, at the opposite end of the city. They're waiting for a home, a room, inside the city, and they multiply while they wait. This is our basic urban problem, but not all of it. Up on the United States border, other hundreds of thousands live in rudimentary shelters, or without shelter, awaiting the day when, they think, they will cross that border. We must build for all of them. Plan! Build! Plan well! Build now!"

A compact fist hits the desk. Scarcely pausing for breath, Pani leans back and asks:

"How fast is traffic moving in Mexico City, today? At fourteen kilometers — nine miles — an hour. Eighty percent of the people who move about travel in twelve percent of the vehicles in use, so the other twenty percent occupy eighty-eight percent of the vehicles. Automobile after automobile, carrying one person, occupying four cubic yards of space! Space." He sighs. "An efficient transportation system — subways are out of the question, too expensive, too impractical here — perhaps monorails to move even a million and a half people daily — would rid the streets of sixty percent of the vehicles that clog them. Mexico City! It has been transformed in one generation. It is spilling over into two States. All these tall buildings!"

His eyes open wide in wonder. "But what is the average height of all the buildings in this city?" A blunt finger stabs the arm of his chair. "One and a half stories." Finger and thumb encompass a tiny space. "One and a half stories!" His tone is scornful. "Make that four stories, or six; house more people, and incidentally give them more space in which to walk." He rises, walks a few steps, breathes deeply. "We must make more superblocks, more cells of twenty thousand or fifty thousand people. Why, automation soon will present us with a twenty-hour working week. Are we prepared for so much leisure? Are we improving, in the cultural sense, so as to use it gracefully? I fear not."

Pani goes back to his chair and asks: "Are all these problems the concern of the architect? Of course they are! People must be housed comfortably, economically. They must have their meeting places, their parks, stores, churches, schools, clinics — and their work — within easy reach, within walking distance as far as is possible. Nowadays, city planning is a professional career in some universities of the United States. The United States is a wonderful, enormous, exciting country, but the planning of new towns, satellite cities, mass housing, is the work of architects. A planner can be educated to investigate the needs of a city, but not to resolve them. After all, the city architect doesn't, cannot, work alone. New uses for new materials demand that he collaborate with whole battalions of technicians. He must constantly extend and renew his lines of communication. He has his field commanders, his designers, draftsmen, mathematicians, contractors, suppliers, endless armies of workers, skilled craftsmen."

Julian Díaz Arias, an engineer, has described Mario Pani as "above all, a man with the capacity to coordinate dissimilar elements so as to realize plans of great social significance. More than anything, he is a statesman, although he has never occupied a public post. His work serves the community, but it is on such a scale that it rises above the field of what is commonly called architecture, and becomes the work of a statesman."

MARIO PANI DARQUI was born in March, 1911, in the then fashionable Santa Maria area of Mexico City. The most curious feature of the neighborhood, and one which he was to remember during the sixteen years of his boyhood and early manhood that he spent in Europe, was a kiosk, placed in a public garden close to his home. It had been built of cast iron, in Chicago, to house the Mexican exhibit at the Paris Exhibition of 1900.

"It was of a curious Moorish design, and dark blue glass in the windows permitted only a minimum of light to enter: which, perhaps, was just as well, since the exhibit was no more representative of Mexico than the building that housed it. That was the way we were, then," he smiles.

At the age of seven Mario said farewell to Mexico City, for in 1918 his father was appointed Mexican Consul-General in Antwerp. The family traveled by railroad to Vera Cruz, to take ship for Europe. The journey, delayed by ambushes, skirmishes and alarums common to the Revolutionary times, took ten days instead of the normal twelve hours.

After only one year in Belgium, Consul-General Pani was posted to Italy and, five years later, to Paris where, in 1925, Mario Pani completed his secondary-school studies, in French. During all these years, his mother was his teacher of the Spanish language and of Mexican history.

On the eve of his nineteenth birthday, Mario decided to study architecture. "Or rather, I agreed to study it. My father and my uncle were civil engineers who, chiefly because of their involvement in politics, had not been able to practice their professions to their satisfaction, and in any case were deeply interested in architecture." He enrolled at l'École des Beaux Arts—"very academic, but certainly the best, and at that time the biggest, with three workshops in the school itself, and ten outside it, run by the students." His first teacher was Georges Gromort. Students at the workshops could enter the central school only by passing highly competitive examinations, and the sixty new members admitted each year included a maximum of fifteen foreigners. Mario failed thrice, but won first place among all the applicants at his fourth attempt. He still believes that this selection on a competitive basis is an ideal system. In the Paris workshops, students of varying ages and grades worked closely together, exchanging ideas and information about the fields in which they were specializing. In later years, he was to resign his Professorship at the School of Archi-

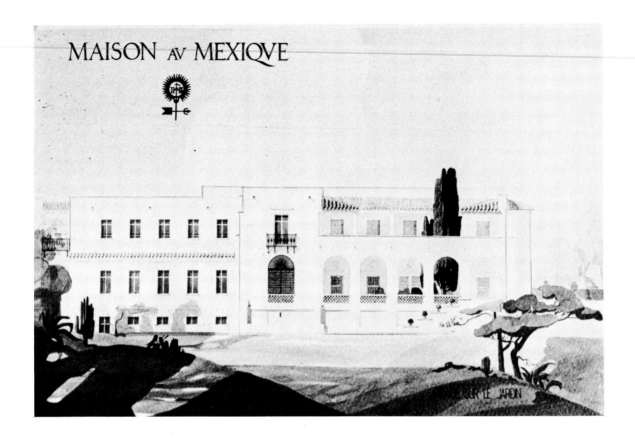

MAISON AV MEXIQVE

tecture of the National University of Mexico "because classes were so big that nobody seemed to benefit from them, and the Beaux Arts type of workshop I introduced was not practicable for that reason."

At the age of eighteen, he had met, while on vacation on the Basque coast, a girl aged thirteen, born in Spain of French and Norwegian parents. At twenty-two, a year before he graduated in 1934, he married her and brought her to his parents' home in Paris. "So, you see, I have been married — most happily married — all my life." Of his four sons and three daughters, the eldest is thirty, the youngest nine, and he is six times a grandfather.

During these formative years, Pani had returned to Mexico only twice: once, while still a child, during an anniversary of Mexican Independence, at the invitation of his uncle, who then was Foreign Secretary: and again in 1933, commissioned by a French firm which did much of the decorative metal work for the Palace of Fine Arts, then being completed in Mexico City. When he came back home, in

1934, "I was quickly made aware that I was not regarded as a true Mexican, having lived most of my life in Europe and having been educated there. Moreover, it seemed that neither did I possess the polish, the grace, that marked a real Frenchman. My only hope was to redeem myself through my work."

In this resolve, luck was not against him. His uncle, Alberto J. Pani, recently Secretary of the Treasury, had planned to build two large hotels and several expensive private homes, and was in disagreement with his chief architect. To the surprise and confusion of almost everybody concerned, these projects were tossed into the lap of the youthful newcomer, who proceeded to design and build, with dispatch and imagination, the first hotel in Mexico City — the Reforma — to cater to the burgeoning tourist industry, and then to add to his collection of scalps the Clasa movie studios. Passionately he insisted, privately and in the public press, that he be allowed to transform the junction of the city's two main avenues, the Paseo de la Reforma and the

Avenida de los Insurgentes, into "a Place d'Étoile, only much bigger, much grander." He pled the cause of a Medical Center, which was to be realized by others in later years, and worked with Jaime Torres Bodet, Secretary of Education under President Manuel Avila Camacho, on a Federal plan for the construction of schools. In this latter project he was successful and active. Area Directors were appointed in every State, and the program as he conceived it and administered it has endured and developed. . . .

And the projects became more numerous, the planning more complicated, the teamwork more effective, the social and architectural significance of the buildings ever greater.

During the late 'thirties Pani entered every competition in which architects were invited to submit plans for monuments, buildings, clubs, stadiums. This, Pani's design for a social and sports club for the Spanish colony in Mexico, was accepted with enthusiasm although the club was not built.

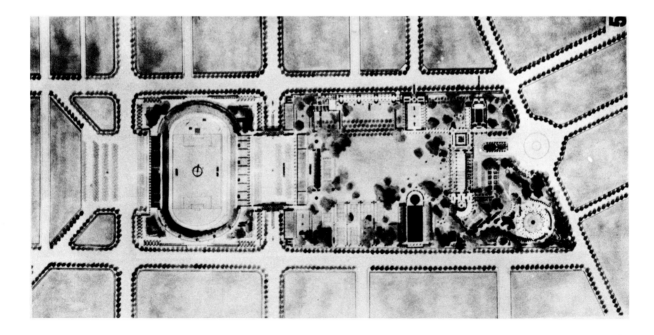

Tlaltelolco

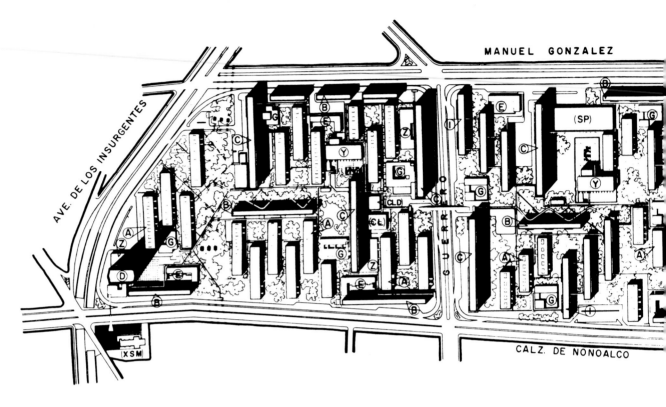

N°			NUMERO DE VIVIENDAS			
TIPO	REC	AREA	UH-1	UH-2	UH-3	TOTAL
A	1	31.81	127		60	91	278
	2	53.59	1433	900	1339		3672
	3	78.34	304		—		304
	3	80.47	168		240	390	798
							5052
B	1	47.86	24		—	40	64
	1	65.73	60		—	100	160
	2	54.68	44		48	16	108
	2	89.59	176		128	128	432
	3	120.21	96		64	96	256
	3	105.24	110		120	40	270
							1290
C	1	48.93	162	162	162		486
	2	91.91	72	72	72		216
	2	99.98	96	96	96		288
	2	102.60	48	48	48		144
	2	103.28	324	324	324		972
	2	132.00	162	162	162		486
							2592

SUMA A-B-C **8,934**
SUMA I-K-L-M-N **2,734**
TOTAL DEPTOS. **11,668**

N°			NUMERO DE VIVIENDAS			
TIPO	REC	AREA	UH-1	UH-2	UH-3	TOTAL
I	1	75.99		126	—	126
	2	73.29		504	—	504
	2	76.88		126	—	126
	3	118.08		126	—	126
	3	121.56		126	—	126
						1006
K	2 PB	167.91		12	12	24
	3	167.18		144	144	288
						312
L	1	46.86		18	72	90
	1	45.40		8	32	40
	1	29.49		8	32	40
	1	43.72		8	32	40
	2	84.88		8	72	90
	2	84.84		8	32	40
	3	101.20		18	72	90
						430
M	2 PB	203.92		6	4	10
	3	103.20		240	160	400
						410
N	2 PB	150.33		—	14	14
	3	81.60		—	560	560
						574

CLAVE.
S.P. SUPER MERCADO
S.T. SECUNDARIA TECNICA
E.P. ESCUELA PREPARATORIA
P.C. PARQUE CENTRAL
S ESCUELA SECUNDARIA

AREA TOTAL	94.45 Ha	100%
AREA VIAL	20.70	22%
AREA UBICACION (sup construido en P B)	26.45	28%
AREA VERDE	47.30	50%

Tlaltelolco

Tlaltelolco is Mario Pani's, Mexico's, Latin America's, perhaps this Continent's, most impressive achievement in urban housing.

It is a town of 70,000 inhabitants. Built on 198 acres, it stands close in to the heart of Mexico City, a forerunner of the Twenty-first Century. Its 11,916 apartments of from one to three bedrooms are contained in 101 buildings that range in height from four to twenty-two stories. An administration and office building, topped by a belfry, is almost the tallest building in Latin America.

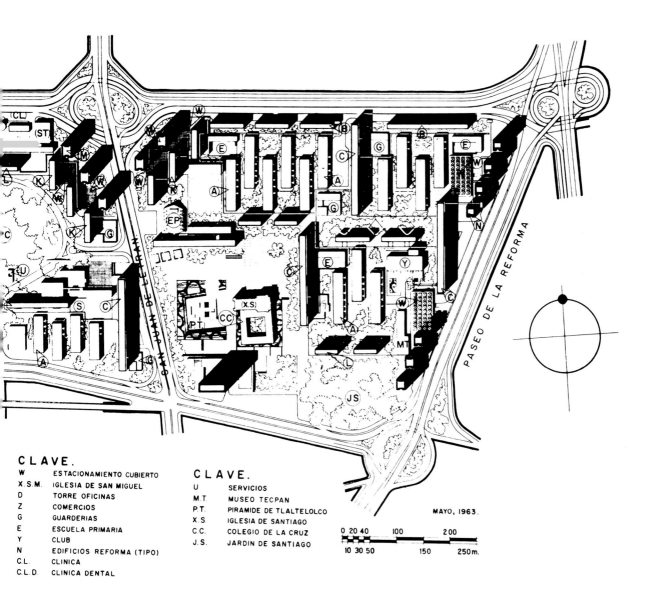

CLAVE.

W	ESTACIONAMIENTO CUBIERTO
X.S.M.	IGLESIA DE SAN MIGUEL
D	TORRE OFICINAS
Z	COMERCIOS
G	GUARDERIAS
E	ESCUELA PRIMARIA
Y	CLUB
N	EDIFICIOS REFORMA (TIPO)
C.L.	CLINICA
C.L.D.	CLINICA DENTAL

CLAVE.

U	SERVICIOS
M.T.	MUSEO TECPAN
P.T.	PIRAMIDE DE TLALTELOLCO
X.S.	IGLESIA DE SANTIAGO
C.C.	COLEGIO DE LA CRUZ
J.S.	JARDIN DE SANTIAGO

MAYO, 1963.

0 20 40   100   200
10 30 50   150   250m.

Tlaltelolco is by no means a crowded town. The built-up area extends over 58.2 acres; roads, streets and paths occupy 45.5 acres; 104 acres are open, green space. The density of population is 902.2 per hectare (2.2 acres).

Tlaltelolco has its own Central Park; three medical or dental clinics; three sports and social clubs; twelve creches; a cinema; multiple shopping areas; subterranean and surface parking lots; a total of thirteen schools — nine primary, two secondary, one secondary technical, one preparatory technical school.

Spanish Colonial architecture is preserved at the southeastern boundary of the town, in the Santiago Church and gardens. Close by, behind the towering new Mexican Secretariat of Foreign Relations, an Aztec pyramid is being restored and the Tecpan Museum is being erected on a site once occupied by the Emperor Cuauhtemoc's palace.

Mario Pani designed and built two of Acapulco's ports of arrival — the airport and the new Yacht Club. (See next page.)

Mario Pani, Sailor

"What am I doing, living up in the mountains and building these cities within cities?" Mario Pani wonders. "Really, I am a man of the sea."

Pani founded the new Acapulco Yacht Club, whose members five times elected him Commodore and, recently, Honorary Commodore. He introduced the first Star sailing boats to Acapulco, and in 1961 bought a cruiser, seventy-six feet in length, built in the United States. Four times he has taken his gleaming, beloved *Santa Cruz* to Los Angeles and back, and it is typical of him that on these voyages he has explored, and to some extent charted, sixteen natural bays on the Pacific and eastern coasts of Lower California. He studies their sources of fresh water, their vegetation, their possibilities as new centers of population and tourism. Above all, he wants to interest United States yachtsmen in them, for their beauty, for the shelter they offer, and as stations for the reception of weather reports and forecasts.

"The sea," he affirms, "is an element, a place, in which to live and to be, not just a means of hopping from one port to another, as they do in the Mediterranean."

The "Los Cocos" apartment building, also a condominium, overlooks Acapulco bay and gives direct access to the beach, a swimming pool and the Yacht Club jetty. Parking for forty-seven automobiles ... ten stores on the mezzanine ... two apartments with private gardens ... eight apartments on a higher floor ... fourteen apartments on the next ... four on the penthouse floor. Associated with Pani in the design of this building, which occupies 3000 square meters, was architect Salvador Ortega.

The Presidente Aleman urban center, built in Mexico City between 1947 and 1949. It comprises 1080 apartments in which live some 5000 people: six three-story buildings; six of thirteen stories. Maximum distance to the nearest of the twenty elevators is thirty meters. The center, which contains a swimming pool, extensive gardens, a crêche, primary schools, stores, and a central laundry, occupies 40,000 square meters.

The Presidente Aleman urban center

The Presidente Aleman urban center

The Presidente Juarez urban center, Mexico City. Nineteen buildings, 984 apartments, housing more than 3000 people. So spacious are the gardens and parks that the density of population is only 137 per hectare, as compared with LeCorbusier's norm of 1000. The center was built in 1950.

The Presidente Juarez urban center

Secretariat of Hydraulic Resources, Mexico City, built between 1946 and 1950. Two of its twenty-two floors are underground.

A ten-story office building, constructed in Mexico City between 1948 and 1950.

196 The first condominium erected in Mexico. Four entrances, from three streets, to the ground floor. The thirteen stories of the larger building contain twenty-two apartments topped by a penthouse. The smaller tower, eight stories high, is an office building.

Begun in 1945 and completed in time to house the Second General Conference of UNESCO in 1947, the National Teachers' College was a worthy forerunner of the University City in Mexican architectural history. The gigantic Olmeca head, cast in concrete, comes from the 1925 archeological find in the State of Tabasco. The College, occupying 120,000 square meters, is on the now built-up Mexico City-Tacuba highway.

The National Conservatory of Music, designed by Pani for the Federal Program for the Construction of Schools, was built in 1945.

Three of a dozen apartment buildings designed and erected in Mexico City in the mid-1940s. (See next page.)

↑
These
Replaced
This
↓

at the Experimental Unit of Popular Housing on the outskirts of Mexico City. Pani and his associates studied the urbanization of a zone in which 12,500 families were to be housed, but only sixty-four houses were constructed.

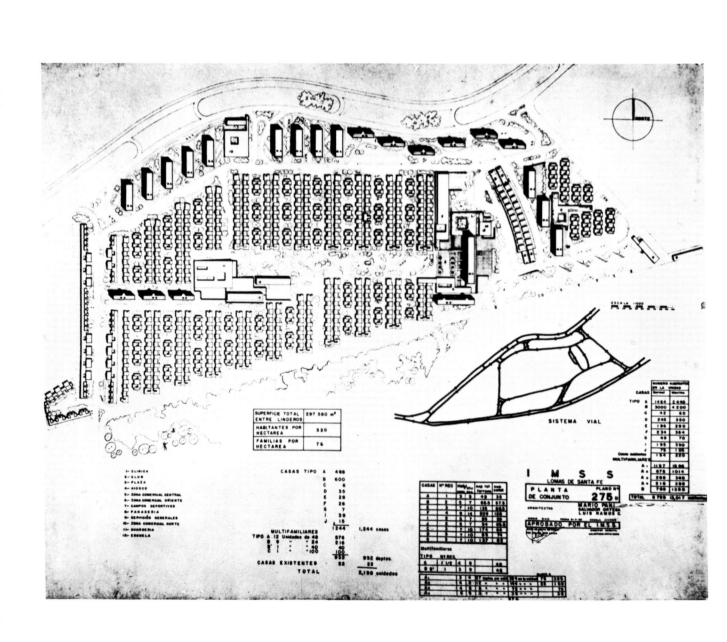

SISTEMA VIAL

SUPERFICIE TOTAL ENTRE LINDEROS	297 560 m²
HABITANTES POR HECTAREA	320
FAMILIAS POR HECTAREA	76

1- CLINICA
2- CLUB
3- PLAZA
4- KIOSCO
5- ZONA COMERCIAL CENTRAL
6- ZONA COMERCIAL ORIENTE
7- CAMPOS DEPORTIVOS
8- PANADERIA
9- SERVICIOS GENERALES
10- ZONA COMERCIAL NORTE
11- GUARDERIA
12- ESCUELA

CASAS TIPO A   486
           B   600
           C   6
           D   35
           E   28
           F   26
           G   7
           I   39
           J   15
                ──────
                1244   1,244 casas

MULTIFAMILIARES
TIPO A 12 Unidades de 48   576
     B 1   " 24   216
     B' 1   " 40   40
     C 1   " 100   100
                    ──────
                    932   932 dptos.
CASAS EXISTENTES   22   22
           TOTAL   2,198 unidades

I M S S
LOMAS DE SANTA FE
PLANTA
DE CONJUNTO   275 b
ARQUITECTOS
MARIO PANI
SALVADOR ORTEGA
LUIS RAMOS G.
APROBADO POR EL I.M.S.S.

The Social Services and Housing Unit of Santa Fe, Mexico City, a complete community of about 14,000 inhabitants, was designed and built for the Mexican Institute of Social Security in 1954-56. It includes a medical clinic, social club, civic square, shopping areas, sports fields, crêches, schools, public gardens, gymnasium, theater and cooperatives for the sale of various articles produced in the complex.

At least five centuries of Mexican social and architectural history here lie exposed— the ruins of Aztec buildings on which the Spaniards built a convent, behind the near-ruins of which rise the multi-windowed towers of the city of Tlaltelolco, built by Mario Pani close to the heart of Mexico City.

Tlaltelco . . .

Tlaltelolco . . .

Tlaltelolco . . .

Tlaltelolco — two views of the tower which houses a campanile

Tlaltelolco

Tlaltelolco

The glass-and-concrete towers of the city-within-a-city do not detract from the almost rural tranquillity of Tlaltelolco's numerous schools.

University City

The land on which Mexico's University City was to be constructed was acquired in 1946, and the Rector of the National University, Dr. Salvador Zubirán, asked Enrique del Moral and José Villagrán García, who then were, respectively, Director and Professor of the National School of Architecture, to make a preliminary, general study. The School then commissioned Enrique del Moral, Mauricio M. Campos and Mario Pani to prepare projects. These were accepted, and in mid-1947 the trio was instructed to develop the over-all plan for the University City. Heavier responsibilities fell upon Del Moral and Pani as a consequence of the death of Mauricio Campos.

Coordination of the multiple, separate construction plans was achieved by periodic meetings with each of the groups of supervising architects. The professional team was the biggest to work on any architectural project in Mexico up to that time. Architects numbered forty — at times, eighty — and engineers and technicians were almost as numerous.

While thus directing the building of a majestic, spacious and functional university, Del Moral and Pani found the time to design the campus, gardens, parking lots, the Rectory, men's dressing rooms, sports fields and — by applying Herrey's theory — the system of internal roads and pathways.

The sports stadium (foreground) and the campus of Mexico's University City.

The Rectory of the National Autonomous University of Mexico.

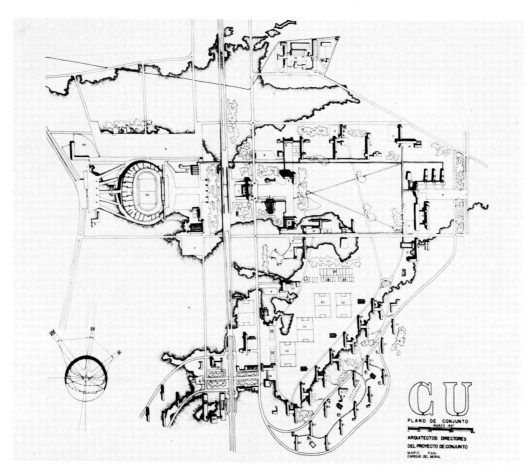

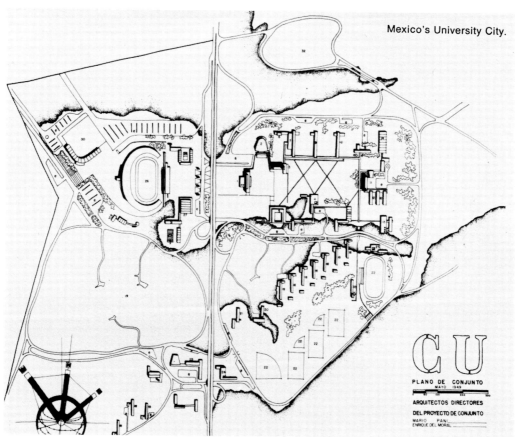

Mexico's University City.

INDEX